# INSPIRATIONS
## FROM
# ANCIENT WISDOM

# INSPIRATIONS
## FROM
# ANCIENT WISDOM

## AT THE FEET
## OF THE MASTER
### BY ALCYONE
### (J. KRISHNAMURTI)

---

## LIGHT ON THE PATH
### AND AN ESSAY ON KARMA
### WRITTEN DOWN BY MABEL COLLINS

---

## THE VOICE OF THE SILENCE
### TRANSLATED AND ANNOTATED
### BY H. P. BLAVATSKY

A publication supported by
THE KERN FOUNDATION

## Quest Books
Theosophical Publishing House

Wheaton, Illinois ◆ Chennai (Madras), India

The Theosophical Publishing House
P.O. Box 270
Wheaton, IL 60189-0270

A publication of the Theosophical Publishing House,
a department of the Theosophical Society in America


Library of Congress Cataloging-in-Publication Data

Inspirations from ancient wisdom / by Alcyone.
     p.   cm.
Contents: At the feet of the Master / by Alcyone
   (J. Krishnamurti)—
Light on the path and an essay on karma written down /
   by Mabel Collins—
The voice of the silence translated and annotated /
   by H. P. Blavatsky.
ISBN 0-8356-0773-9
     1. Spiritual life.   2. Theosophy.   I. Krishnamurti,
J. (Jiddu), 1895–1986. At the feet of the Master.   II. Collins,
Mabel, 1851–1927. Light on the path.   III. Blavatsky, H. P.
(Helena Petrovna), 1831–1891. Voice of the silence.
BL624.I56   1999
299'.934—dc21                           98-36865
                                              CIP

5  4  3  2  1  *  99  00  01  02  03  04  05  06

Printed in the United States of America

# CONTENTS

# PUBLISHER'S FOREWORD

*Inspirations from Ancient Wisdom* presents for the general reader three small works that are classics in the modern Theosophical expression of the timeless Wisdom Tradition. All three are about how to travel the Path, that is, to live so as to become a complete human being.

These works were originally published between 1885 and 1910. They are thus now about a hundred years old. Their content is timeless, but the language in which they were originally published is dated in certain ways. Language, like everything else in this world, is constantly changing. In this edition, we have therefore somewhat modernized the wording, punctuation, spelling, and other such matters of format, without affecting the sense of the original.

*At the Feet of the Master* needed the least modernization, being the most recent of the texts and written in a plain style. *Light on the Path* received the most modernization, as an older work with a complex internal structure and considerable variation in its style. *The Voice of the Silence*, although nearly as old as *Light on the Path* in its first publication, is as a whole more ancient in style than the latter, and its style is so much a part of the book that it has been thought better to be restrained in modernizing it; consequently very few changes have been introduced into this work.

The present edition is intended for contemporary readers interested in applying to their lives the wisdom set forth in these books. For students with a historical interest as well, the original texts are and will remain in print. In addition, the original texts are available from Quest Books on three audio cassettes: *At the Feet of the Master* and *Light on the Path* read by Broadway, Hollywood, and television actress Dana Ivey, and *The Voice of the Silence* read by actor-director-teacher Paul Meier.

# INTRODUCTION

"Our hearts are ever restless," wrote St. Augustine, "until they find their rest in thee."

In that opening confession of his spiritual autobiography, the greatest of the Latin Fathers of the Church set forth a universal principle in Christian terms. Spiritual traditions all over the world recognize that human beings are creatures with restless hearts. We are not content to be just content. Dogs, cats, bumblebees, and whales do not—so far as we know—pine to be something other than what they are. They accept their dogginess or whaleship.

The human animal, on the other hand, is by nature discontent. We want to be somewhere we are not or to become something we are not. We have implanted in our breasts a divine discontent that moves us. We seek salvation, liberation, enlightenment, transformation, regeneration, the Kingdom of Heaven, the Pure Land, Übermenschheit—we call it many things. But under whatever name, it is something other and greater than the ordinary everyday round of existence.

The British author Francis Thompson wrote of the restless heart under the image of a pursuit in his poem "The Hound of Heaven":

> I fled Him, down the nights and down the days;
>   I fled Him, down the arches of the years;
> I fled Him, down the labyrinthine ways
>   Of my own mind; and in the mist of tears
> I hid from Him, and under running laughter.

The Buddha also spoke of our restless heart in his four Noble Truths. In the first Truth, he called the experience of a restless heart *duhkha*—sorrow, grief, or frustration. In the second, he identified the cause of that experience—the craving for what we do not have or are not. In the third, he pointed to the rest we seek as *nirvana*—the blowing out of all restlessness. And in the fourth, he affirmed the existence of a Path to that rest.

Spiritual traditions all over the world have offered roadmaps for the restless heart to find its rest in God, nirvana, or whatever we may call the end of our seeking. The Sermon on the Mount is such a roadmap, and so are the Bhagavad Gita, the Dhammapada, the Tao Te Ching, the *Spiritual Exercises* of Ignatius Loyola, and many another little book. The modern Theosophical tradition has three such roadmaps, for differing needs and sensibilities: *At the Feet of the Master*, *Light on the Path*, and *The Voice of the Silence*.

We need more than one roadmap for our spiritual journey because, as the General Semanticist

Alfred Korzybski pointed out, the map is not the territory. Different maps show different things about the same territory or the same road. One of the Theosophical roadmaps, *The Voice of the Silence*, advises the traveler: "Prepare thyself, for thou wilt have to travel on alone. The Teacher can but point the way. The Path is one for all, the means to reach the goal must vary with the Pilgrims."

It is a paradox. There is a Path. It is described by the many different roadmaps of spiritual traditions all over the world. Yet the goal of that Path is what Jiddu Krishnamurti called "a pathless land." That paradox has been long known. It is observed in guidebooks like *The Voice* and by other traditions that seek to comfort the restless heart. Thus, in one of the Degrees of Freemasonry, the candidate is told that he must "plunge in all humility into the mysterious and glorious depths of his own inmost being, if he would win the Light he seeks; for each must find that Hidden Glory for himself, as all the Children of the Light have found it."

There is a "Hidden Glory" and a place where that Glory lies concealed. There is also a way to that place, but we must each find it for ourselves. And that is why there are many roadmaps, not one only. Each map treats a different stage or aspect of the journey. And we each experience the journey in our own ways. Yet, even though the map is not the territory, maps are useful things—provided we do not mistake what they are and what they are good for.

The three Theosophical guidebooks or roadmaps address different aspects of our journey. They are inevitably similar because they are concerned with the same experience, although each views that experience from a different standpoint and so in its own unique way. Collectively these three books are complementary, providing a sequential course of spiritual development.

*At the Feet of the Master* is preparatory, dealing with what comes first. It answers the question "How do I prepare to walk the Path?"

*Light on the Path* is progressive, being concerned with what the Path itself is like. It answers the question "What will I find as I walk the Path?"

*The Voice of the Silence* is cumulative, leading up to what comes at the end of the Path. It answers the question "Where does the Path lead?"

For each of these three little books, we may consider briefly something about how it was written, what character it has, what its structure is, and what its message to us may be.

## At the Feet of the Master

Jiddu Krishnamurti was a Brahmin boy thirteen years of age when his father began to work on the Theosophical campus at Adyar, near Madras, India. There the boy was noticed by C. W. Leadbeater, a former Anglican clergyman who had become a leading figure in the Theosophical Society and who recognized in the young ragamuffin, quite improbably, a great spiritual potential. Leadbeater consequently assumed responsibility for the boy's education, including instruction in English, cleanliness, Western manners, and spiritual progress.

As part of his spiritual education, the young Krishnamurti was taught during his sleep at night by one of the advanced beings known as "mahatmas" or "masters of the Wisdom." At the end of each nightly session, the teacher summarized the basic points of the instruction in a few sentences of simple language. Each morning when the boy awoke, he would write down what he remembered of the previous night's teaching. The English, spelling, and punctuation were corrected, but otherwise the substance of the material was not changed. What Krishnamurti wrote was gathered together and published in 1910 as *At the Feet of the Master*. The pen name of "Alcyone" under which the book appeared is the "star name" of Krishnamurti, alluding to his higher Self.

The title of the book is also noteworthy. In the philosophical tradition of India, instructions in the Vedanta tradition are called Upanishads. The word *Upanishad* means literally "sitting down near to (the teacher)," that is, "at the feet of the master." The historical Upanishads deal, however, with great metaphysical principles, while this little book treats the practical problems of daily living on the spiritual path. It is intended as simple guidance to right behavior—the prerequisite for any spiritual progress.

The four parts of the book set forth in modern language four ancient qualifications for entering the path. Here they are called (1) discrimination or choosing rightly, (2) desirelessness or viewing rightly,

(3) good conduct or acting rightly, and (4) love or responding rightly. Together they tell us how to prepare ourselves to walk the Path.

# Light on the Path

*Light on the Path* was first published in 1885, twenty-five years before *At the Feet of the Master*. It was written down by Mabel Collins, a prolific author of the last century. She wrote long three-volume romances for the popular trade and short spiritual works for a more restricted readership. The former were potboilers; the latter were in some sense "inspired." Of the shorter works, the most influential and clearly the most inspired is *Light on the Path*.

*Light on the Path* has three levels of material. At its core are thirty short aphoristic and often enigmatic "rules," each of which is an injunction or order to do something. These injunctions are divided into ten sets of three each, and further the ten sets are grouped into two halves of fifteen injunctions (five sets) each. Certain themes unite the rules in each set and each half, and these themes also distinguish the sets and halves from each other. The language of the "rules" seems ancient and spare.

The second level of the book consists of amplifications of the thirty rules. The amplified statements are more discursive than the "rules," but like the "rules" are expressed in a style that is somewhat archaic. The amplifications are poetic with high rhetorical embellishments. The third level is a series of more prosaic notes or commentaries. They are distinctly plainer in style and more contemporary.

The first six "rules" tell us to kill out desire for various things that seem to be normal parts of life. The next six "rules" tell us, paradoxically, to desire various things. The following three "rules," which complete the first half of the book, enjoin us to seek the way—a way that resolves the paradox of the first twelve "rules." This half is especially for those who are just setting their feet upon the Path.

The second half gives directions for progressing on that Path. The first three "rules" use the metaphor of a warrior; the second set of three uses the metaphor of music. The contrast between these two metaphors echoes a similar contrast in the Bhagavad Gita, the great spiritual guidebook of India, which is about a war but whose title means "The Song of the Blessed One." The third set of "rules" urges us to look around us and within ourselves; the fourth set instructs us to inquire about secrets that the looking may reveal to us; the final set concerns our response to those secrets.

The book ends with a short essay on "Karma," which is usually printed with it and has important implications for carrying out the "rules."

## The Voice of the Silence

*The Voice of the Silence* was published by H. P. Blavatsky in 1889, just four years after *Light on the Path*. It consists of 316 verses, ranging in length from several words to a few sentences. The verses are in three "fragments," which Blavatsky says are extracts from a longer work called *The Book of the Golden Precepts*, another of the spiritual guidebooks.

All three fragments are about the journey a pilgrim makes on the Path of spiritual development. Each of the fragments treats that journey in a somewhat different way, but all three are focused on what lies at the end of the Path—the purpose for treading it.

The first fragment, "The Voice of the Silence," from which the whole book takes its title, speaks of the Path metaphorically as a passage through three halls: the Hall of Ignorance, the Hall of Learning, and the Hall of Wisdom, into the Vale of Bliss beyond them all. It also speaks of hearing the Voice of the Silence in seven manners: as a nightingale, a silver cymbal, an ocean shell, a stringed instrument, a bamboo flute, a trumpet, and a thundercloud. The last is succeeded by silence—the Voice of the Silence. Those seven manners are symbolic of seven aspects of our own nature and thus of seven "initiations" on the Path or seven stages that lead to the eighth—the end of the journey, the Vale of Bliss that lies beyond the Hall of Wisdom.

The second fragment, "The Two Paths," talks about a fork in the road, at which we must decide which of two directions we will travel. One direction leads to benefit for ourselves; the other leads to personal self-sacrifice for the welfare of all humanity. The second direction is that of the bodhisattvas, those saintly figures whose essence is wisdom and who have dedicated themselves to the service of all life.

The third fragment, "The Seven Portals," continues the theme of the second fragment in celebrating dedication to the good of all humanity as the highest ideal of life. Its central metaphor is the passage of seven gates or portals, each being opened by a key that is one of the transcendental virtues: charity, harmony, patience, clear-sightedness, courage, contemplation, and wisdom.

The book ends with an ecstatic celebration of what it means—not just to arrive at the end of the Path, where the restless heart finds peace—but to return from that peace to help others along the way. Or in a different metaphor, to cross to the other shore of life and then come back to this shore. The final words allude to the theme of the Voice of the Silence, for a "wordless voice" speaks. What it says can be lightly paraphrased:

> All Nature's wordless voice in thousand tones arises to proclaim: Joy unto you, O people of Earth. A pilgrim has returned back from the other shore. A new saint is born. Peace to all beings.

—John Algeo

# At the Feet
## of the Master
by Alcyone (J. Krishnamurti)

# FOREWORD

## by Annie Besant

The privilege is given to me, as an elder, to pen a word of introduction to this little book, the first written by a younger brother, young in body verily, but not in soul. The teachings contained in it were given to him by his Master in preparing him for initiation, and were written down by him from memory—slowly and laboriously, for his English last year was far less fluent than it is now. The greater part is a reproduction of the Master's own words; that which is not such a verbal reproduction is the Master's thought clothed in his pupil's words. Two omitted sentences were supplied by the Master. In two other cases an omitted word has been added. Beyond this, it is entirely Alcyone's own, his first gift to the world.

May it help others as the spoken teachings helped him—such is the hope with which he gives it. But the teaching can only be fruitful if it is *lived*, as he has lived it, since it fell from the Master's lips. If the example be followed as well as the precept, then for the reader, as for the writer, shall the great portal swing open, and his feet be set on the path.

## To Those Who Knock

From the unreal lead me to the Real.
From darkness lead me to Light.
From death lead me to Immortality.

# PREFACE

These are not my words; they are the words of the Master who taught me. Without him I could have done nothing, but through his help I have set my feet upon the path. You also desire to enter the same path, so the words which he spoke to me will help you also, if you will obey them. It is not enough to say that they are true and beautiful; anyone who wishes to succeed must do exactly what is said. To look at food and say that it is good will not satisfy a starving man; he must put forth his hand and eat. So to hear the Master's words is not enough; you must do what he says, attending to every word, taking every hint. If a hint is not taken, if a word is missed, it is lost forever; for he does not speak twice.

Four qualifications there are for this pathway:

> Discrimination
> Desirelessness
> Good Conduct
> Love

What the Master has said to me on each of these I shall try to tell you.

> — Alcyone

# PART ONE

# Discrimination

The first of these qualifications is discrimination, and this is usually taken as the discrimination between the real and the unreal which leads you to enter the path. It is this, but it is also much more; and it is to be practiced, not only at the beginning of the path, but at every step of it every day until the end. You enter the path because you have learned that on it alone can be found those things that are worth gaining. People who do not know work to gain wealth and power, but these are at most for one life only and therefore unreal. There are greater things than these—things that are real and lasting; when you have once seen these, you desire those others no more.

In the entire world there are only two kinds of people—those who know and those who do not know; and this knowledge is the thing which matters. What religion we hold, to what race we belong—these things are not important; the really important thing is this knowledge—the knowledge of God's plan for us. For God has a plan and that plan is evolution. When once we have seen that and really know it, we cannot help working for it and making ourselves one with it, because it is so glorious, so beautiful. So, because we know, we are on God's side, standing for good and resisting evil, working for evolution and not for selfishness.

If you are on God's side, you are one of us, and it does not matter in the least whether you call yourself a Hindu, or a Buddhist, a Christian or a Muslim, whether you are from India or England, China or Russia. Those who are on God's side know why they are here and what they should do, and they are trying to do it; all the others do not yet know what they should do, and so often act foolishly, and try to invent ways for themselves which they think will be pleasant for themselves, not understanding that all are one, and that therefore only what the One wills can ever be really pleasant for anyone. They are following the unreal instead of the real. Until they learn to distinguish between these two, they have not ranged themselves on God's side, and so this discrimination is the first step.

But even when the choice is made, you must still remember that of the real and the unreal there are many varieties; and discrimination must still be made between the right and the wrong, the important and the unimportant, the useful and the useless, the true and the false, the selfish and the unselfish.

Between right and wrong it should not be difficult to choose, for those who wish to follow the

Master have already decided to take the right at all costs. But you and your body are two, and your will is not always what your body wishes. When your body wishes something, stop and think whether *you* really wish it. For *you* are God, and you will only what God wills; but you must dig deep down into yourself to find the God within you, and listen to his voice, which is *your* voice. Do not mistake your bodies for yourself—neither the physical body, nor the astral, nor the mental. Each one of them will pretend to be the Self, in order to gain what it wants. But you must know them all and know yourself as their master.

When there is work that must be done, the physical body wants to rest, to go out walking, to eat and drink; and the person who does not know says, "*I* want to do these things, and I must do them." But the person who knows says, "This that wants it is *not* I, and it must wait awhile." Often when there is an opportunity to help someone, the body feels: "How much trouble it will be for me; let someone else do it." But you must reply to your body: "You shall not hinder me in doing good work."

The body is your animal—the horse upon which you ride. Therefore you must treat it well, and take good care of it; you must not overwork it; you must feed it properly on pure food and drink only, and keep it strictly clean always, even from the minutest speck of dirt. For without a perfectly clean and healthy body you cannot do the arduous work of preparation, you cannot bear its ceaseless strain. But it must always be you who control that body, not it that controls you.

The astral body has *its* desires—dozens of them; it wants you to be angry, to say sharp words, to feel jealous, to be greedy for money, to envy other people their possessions, to yield yourself to depression. All these things it wants, and many more, not because it wishes to harm you, but because it likes violent vibrations, and likes to change them constantly. But *you* want none of these things, and therefore you must discriminate between your wants and your body's.

Your mental body wishes to think itself proudly separate, to think much of itself and little of others. Even when you have turned it away from worldly things, it still tries to calculate for self, to make you think of your own progress, instead of thinking of the Master's work and of helping others. When you meditate, it will try to make you think of the many different things which *it* wants instead of the one thing which *you* want. You are not this mind, but it is yours to use; so here again discrimination is necessary. You must watch unceasingly, or you will fail.

Between right and wrong, the wisdom teachings know no compromise. At whatever apparent cost, that which is right you must do, that which is wrong you must not do, no matter what the ignorant may think or say. You must study deeply the hidden laws of Nature, and when you know them arrange your life according to them, always using reason and common sense.

You must discriminate between the important and the unimportant. Firm as a rock where right and wrong are concerned, yield always to others in things that do not matter. For you must be always gentle and kindly, reasonable and accommodating, leaving to others the same full liberty that you need for yourself.

Try to see what is worth doing, and remember that you must not judge by the size of a thing. A small thing which is directly useful in the Master's work is far better worth doing than a large thing which the world would call good. You must distinguish not only the useful from the useless, but the more useful from the less useful. To feed the poor is a good and noble and useful work; yet to feed their souls is nobler and more useful than to feed their bodies. Any rich person can feed the body, but only those who know can feed the soul. If you know, it is your duty to help others to know.

However wise you may be already, on this path you have much to learn; so much that here also there must be discrimination, and you must think carefully what is worth learning. All knowledge is useful, and one day you will have all knowledge; but while you have only part, take care that it is the most useful part. God is wisdom as well as love, and the more wisdom you have the more you can manifest of God. Study then, but study first that which will most help you to help others. Work patiently at your studies, not that others may think you wise, not even that you may have the happiness of being wise, but because only the wise person can be wisely helpful. However much you wish to help, if you are ignorant you may do more harm than good.

You must distinguish between truth and falsehood; you must learn to be true all through, in thought and word and deed.

In thought first, and that is not easy, for there are in the world many untrue thoughts, many foolish superstitions, and no one who is enslaved by them can make progress. Therefore you must not hold a thought just because many other people hold it, nor because it has been believed for centuries, nor because it is written in some book which people think sacred; you must think of the matter for yourself, and judge for yourself whether it is reasonable. Remember that though a thousand people agree upon a subject, if they know nothing about that subject their opinion is of no value. You who would walk upon the path must learn to think for yourself, for superstition is one of the greatest evils in the world, one of the fetters from which you must utterly free yourself.

Your thought about others must be true; you must not think of them what you do not know. Do not suppose that they are always thinking of you. If people do something which you think will harm you, or say something which you think applies to you, do not think at once: "They meant to injure me." Most probably they never thought of you at all, for each soul has its own troubles and its thoughts turn chiefly around itself. If people speak angrily to you, do not think: "They hate me, they wish to wound me." Probably someone or something else has made them angry, and because they happen to meet you they turn their anger upon you. They are acting foolishly, for all anger is foolish, but you must not therefore think untruly of them.

When you become a pupil of the Master, you may always try the truth of your thought by laying it beside his. For the pupil is one with the Master, and needs only to put back his thought into the Master's thought to see at once whether it agrees. If it does not, it is wrong, and the pupil changes it instantly, for the Master's thought is perfect, because he knows all. Those who are not yet accepted by him cannot do quite this, but they may greatly help themselves by stopping often to think: "What would the Master think about this? What would the Master say or do under these circumstances?" For you must never do or say or think what you cannot imagine the Master as doing or saying or thinking.

You must be true in speech too—accurate and without exaggeration. Never attribute motives to another; only the Master knows the pupil's thoughts, and he may be acting from reasons which have never entered your mind. If you hear a story against anyone, do not repeat it; it may not be true, and even if it is, it is kinder to say nothing. Think well before speaking, lest you should fall into inaccuracy.

Be true in action; never pretend to be other than you are, for all pretense is a hindrance to the pure light of truth, which should shine through you as sunlight shines through clear glass.

You must discriminate between the selfish and the unselfish. For selfishness has many forms, and when you think you have finally killed it in one of them, it arises in another as strongly as ever. But by degrees you will become so full of thought for the helping of others that there will be no room, no time, for any thought about yourself.

You must discriminate in yet another way. Learn to distinguish the God in everyone and everything, no matter how evil they may appear on the surface. You can help your brothers and sisters through that which you have in common with them, and that is the Divine Life; learn how to arouse that in them, learn how to appeal to that in them, and so shall you save your brothers and sisters from wrong.

# PART TWO
## Desirelessness

There are many for whom the qualification of desirelessness is a difficult one, for they feel that they *are* their desires—that if their distinctive desires, their likings and dislikings, are taken away from them, there will be no self left. But these are only the ones who have not seen the Master; in the light of his holy presence all desire dies but the desire to be like him. Yet before you have the happiness of meeting him face to face, you may attain desirelessness if you will. Discrimination has already shown you that the things which most people desire, such as wealth and power, are not worth having; when this is really felt, not merely said, all desire for them ceases.

Thus far all is simple; it needs only that you should understand. But there are some who forsake the pursuit of earthly aims only in order to gain heaven, or to attain personal liberation from rebirth; into this error you must not fall. If you have forgotten self altogether, you cannot be thinking when that self should be set free, or what kind of heaven it shall have. Remember that *all* selfish desire binds, however high may be its object, and until you have gotten rid of it you are not wholly free to devote yourself to the work of the Master.

When all desires for self are gone, there may still be a desire to see the result of your work. If you help anybody, you want to *see* how much you have helped them; perhaps even you want them to see it too, and to be grateful. But this is still desire, and also want of trust. When you pour out your strength to help, there must be a result, whether you can see it or not; if you know the law you know this must be so. So you must do right for the sake of the right, not in the hope of reward; you must work for the sake of the work, not in the hope of seeing the result; you must give yourself to the service of the world because you love it and cannot help giving yourself to it.

Have no desire for psychic powers; they will come when the Master knows that it is best for you to have them. To force them too soon often brings in its train much trouble; often their possessor is misled by deceitful nature spirits, or becomes conceited and thinks he cannot make a mistake; and in any case the time and strength that it takes to gain them might be spent in work for others. They will come in the course of development—they *must* come; and if the Master sees that it would be useful for you to have them sooner, he will tell you how to unfold them safely. Until then, you are better without them.

You must guard, too, against certain small desires which are common in daily life. Never wish to shine or to appear clever; have no desire to speak. It is well to speak little; better still to say nothing, unless you are quite sure that what you wish to say is true, kind, and helpful. Before speaking think carefully whether what you are going to say has those three qualities; if it has not, do not say it.

It is well even now to get used to thinking carefully before speaking; for when you reach initiation you must watch every word, lest you should tell what must not be told. Much common talk is unnecessary and foolish; when it is gossip, it is wicked. So be accustomed to listen rather than talk; do not offer opinions unless directly asked for them. One statement of the qualifications gives them thus: to know, to dare, to will, and to be silent; and the last of the four is the hardest of them all.

Another common desire that you must sternly repress is the wish to meddle in other people's business. What others do or say or believe is no affair of yours, and you must learn to let them absolutely alone. They have full right to free thought and speech and action, so long as they do not interfere with anyone else. You yourself claim the freedom to do what you think proper; you must allow the same freedom to others, and when they exercise it you have no right to talk about them.

If you think someone is doing wrong, and you can contrive an opportunity to privately and very politely tell them why you think so, it is possible that you may convince them; but there are many cases in which even that would be an improper interference. On no account must you gossip to some third person about the matter, for that is an extremely wicked action.

If you see a case of cruelty to a child or an animal, it is your duty to interfere. If you see anyone breaking the law of the country, you should inform the authorities. If you are placed in charge of another person in order to teach him, it may become your duty gently to tell him of his faults. Except in such cases, mind your own business and learn the virtue of silence.

## PART THREE

## Good Conduct

The six points of conduct which are especially required are given by the Master as:

1. Self-control as to the mind
2. Self-control in action
3. Tolerance
4. Cheerfulness
5. One-pointedness
6. Confidence

[I know some of these are often translated differently, as are the names of the qualifications; but in all cases I am using the names which the Master himself employed when explaining them to me.]

1. *Self-control as to the mind*. The qualification of desirelessness shows that the astral body must be controlled; this shows the same thing as to the mental body. It means control of temper, so that you may feel no anger or impatience; of the mind itself, so that the thought may always be calm and unruffled; and

(through the mind) of the nerves, so that they may be as little irritable as possible. This last is difficult, because when you try to prepare yourself for the path, you cannot help making your body more sensitive, so that its nerves are easily disturbed by a sound or a shock and feel any pressure acutely; but you must do your best.

The calm mind means also courage, so that you may face without fear the trials and difficulties of the path; it means also steadiness, so that you may make light of the troubles which come into everyone's life, and avoid the incessant worry over little things in which many people spend most of their time. The Master teaches that it does not matter in the least what happens to you from the outside: sorrows, troubles, sicknesses, losses—all these must be as nothing to you and must not be allowed to affect the calmness of your mind. They are the result of past actions, and when they come you must bear them cheerfully, remembering that all evil is transitory and that your duty is to remain always joyous and serene. They belong to your previous lives, not to this; you cannot alter them, so it is useless to trouble about them. Think rather of what you are doing now, which will make the events of your next life, for that you *can* alter.

Never allow yourself to feel sad or depressed. Depression is wrong, because it infects others and makes their lives harder, which you have no right to do. Therefore if ever it comes to you, throw it off at once.

In yet another way you must control your thought: you must not let it wander. Whatever you are doing, fix your thought upon it, that it may be perfectly done. Do not let your mind be idle, but keep good thoughts always in the background of it, ready to come forward the moment it is free.

Use your thought power every day for good purposes; be a force in the direction of evolution. Think each day of someone whom you know to be in sorrow, or suffering, or in need of help, and pour out loving thought upon them.

Hold back your mind from pride, for pride comes only from ignorance. Those who do not know think that they are great, that they have done this or that great thing; the wise know that only God is great, that all good work is done by God alone.

2. *Self-control in action.* If your thought is what it should be, you will have little trouble with your action. Yet remember that, to be useful to others, thought must result in action. There must be no laziness, only constant activity in good work. But it must be your *own* duty that you do—not another's, unless with their permission and by way of helping them. Leave others to do their own work in their own way; be always ready to offer help where it is needed, but *never* interfere. For many people the most difficult thing in the world to learn is to mind their own business, but that is exactly what you must do.

Because you try to take up higher work, you must not forget your ordinary duties, for until they are done you are not free for other service. You should undertake no new worldly duties; but those which you have already taken upon you, you must perfectly fulfill—all clear and reasonable duties which you yourself recognize, that is, not imaginary duties which others try to impose upon you. If you are to be God's, you must do ordinary work better than others, not worse; because you must do that also for God's sake.

3. *Tolerance.* You must feel perfect tolerance for all and a hearty interest in the beliefs of those of another religion, just as much as in your own. For their religion is a path to the highest, just as yours is. And to help all, you must understand all.

But in order to gain this perfect tolerance, you must yourself first be free from bigotry and superstition. You must learn that no ceremonies are necessary, else you will think yourself somehow better than those who do not perform them. Yet you must not condemn others who still cling to ceremonies. Let them do as they will; however they must not interfere with you who know the truth—they must not try to force upon you that which you have outgrown. Make allowance for everything; be kindly towards everything.

Now that your eyes are opened, some of your old beliefs, your old ceremonies, may seem absurd to you; perhaps, indeed, they really are so. Yet though you can no longer take part in them, respect them for the sake of those good souls to whom they are still important. They have their place; they have their use; they are like those double lines which guided you as a child to write straight and evenly, until you learned to write far better and more freely without them. There was a time when you needed them, but now that time is past.

A great Teacher once wrote: "When I was a child, I spake as a child, I understood as a child, I thought as a child; but when I became a man I put away childish things." Yet the person who has forgotten his childhood and lost sympathy with the children is not the one who can teach them or help them. So look kindly, gently, tolerantly upon all, but upon all alike: Buddhist or Hindu, Jain or Jew, Christian or Muslim.

4. *Cheerfulness.* You must bear your karma cheerfully, whatever it may be, taking it as an honor that suffering comes to you, because it shows that the Lords of Karma think you worth helping. However hard it is, be thankful that it is no worse. Remember that you are of but little use to the Master until your evil karma is worked out, and you are free. By offering yourself to him, you have asked that your karma may be hurried, and so now in one or two lives you work through what otherwise might have been spread over a hundred. But in order to make the best out of it, you must bear it cheerfully, gladly.

Yet another point. You must give up all feeling of possession. Karma may take from you the things that you like best—even the people whom you love most. Even then you must be cheerful—ready to part with anything and everything. Often the Master needs to pour out his strength upon others through his servant; he cannot do that if the servant yields to depression. So cheerfulness must be the rule.

5. *One-pointedness.* The one thing that you must set before you is to do the Master's work. Whatever else may come in your way to do, that at least you must never forget. Yet nothing else *can* come in your way, for all helpful, unselfish work is the Master's work, and you must do it for his sake. And you must give all your attention to each piece as you do it, so that it may be your very best. The same Teacher also wrote: "Whatsoever ye do, do it *heartily*, as to the Lord, and not unto men." Think how you would do a piece of work if you knew that the Master was coming at once to look at it; just in that way you must do all your work. Those who know most will most understand all that that verse means. And there is another like it, much older: "Whatsoever thy hand findeth to do, do it with thy might."

One-pointedness means, too, that nothing shall ever turn you, even for a moment, from the path upon which you have entered. No temptations, no worldly pleasures, no worldly affections even, must ever draw you aside. For you yourself must become one with the path; it must be so much part of your nature that you follow it without needing to think of it and cannot turn aside. You, the monad, have decided it; to break away from it would be to break away from yourself.

6. *Confidence.* You must trust your Master; you must trust yourself. If you have seen the Master, you will trust him to the uttermost, through many lives and deaths. If you have not yet seen him, you must still try to realize him and trust him, because if you do not, even he cannot help you. Unless there is perfect

trust, there cannot be the perfect flow of love and power.

You must trust yourself. You say you know yourself too well? If you feel so, you do *not* know yourself; you know only the weak outer husk, which has fallen often into the mire. But *you*—the real you—you are a spark of God's own fire, and God, who is almighty, is in you, and because of that there is nothing that you cannot do if you will. Say to yourself: "What man has done, man can do. I am a man, yet also God in man; I can do this thing, and I will." For your will must be like tempered steel, if you would tread the path.

# PART FOUR

## Love

Of all the qualifications, love is the most important, for if it is strong enough in us, it forces us to acquire all the rest, and all the rest without it would never be sufficient. Often it is translated as an intense desire for liberation from the round of births and deaths and for union with God. But to put it in that way sounds selfish and gives only part of the meaning. It is not so much desire as *will*, resolve, determination. To produce its result, this resolve must fill your whole nature, so as to leave no room for any other feeling. It is indeed the will to be one with God, not in order that you may escape from weariness and suffering, but in order that because of your deep love you may act with God and as God does. Because God is Love, you, if you would become one with God, must be filled with perfect unselfishness and love also.

In daily life this means two things: first, that you shall be careful to do no harm to any living thing; second, that you shall always be watching for an opportunity to help.

First, to do no hurt. There are three sins which work more harm than all else in the world— gossip, cruelty, and superstition—because they are sins against love. Against these three those who would fill their hearts with the love of God must watch ceaselessly.

See what gossip does. It begins with evil thought, and that in itself is a crime. For in everyone and in everything there is good; in everyone and in everything there is evil. Either of these we can strengthen by thinking of it, and in this way we can help or hinder evolution; we can do the will of the Logos or we can resist it. If you think of the evil in another, you are doing at the same time three wicked things:

(1) You are filling your neighborhood with evil thought instead of with good thought, and so you are adding to the sorrow of the world.

(2) If there is in that person the evil that you imagine, you are strengthening it and feeding it, and so you are making that person worse instead of better. But generally the evil is not there, and you have only fancied it; then your wicked thoughts tempt those around you to do wrong, for if they are not yet perfect you may make them that which you have thought them.

(3) You fill your own mind with evil thoughts instead of good, and so you hinder your own growth, and make yourself, for those who can see, an ugly and painful object instead of a beautiful and lovable one.

Not content with having done all this harm to themselves and their victims, gossips try with all their might to make other people partners in crime. Eagerly the gossiper tells a wicked tale to others, hoping that they will believe them; and then they join with the gossiper in pouring evil thoughts upon the poor sufferer. And this goes on day after day and is done not by one person but by thousands. Do you begin to see how base, how terrible a sin this is? You must avoid it altogether. Never speak ill of anyone; refuse to listen when anyone else speaks ill of another but gently say: "Perhaps this is not true, and even if it is, it is kinder not to speak of it."

Then as to cruelty. This is of two kinds, intentional and unintentional. Intentional cruelty is purposely to give pain to another living being, and that is the greatest of all sins—the work of a devil rather than a human being. You might think that no person could do such a thing, but people have done it often, and are daily doing it now. The inquisitors did it; many religious people did it in the name of their religion. Vivisectionists do it; many teachers do it habitually. All these people try to excuse their brutality by saying that it is the custom, but a crime does not cease to be a crime because many commit it. Karma takes no account of custom, and the karma of cruelty is the most terrible of all. In India at least there can be no excuse for such customs, for the duty of harmlessness is well known to all. The fate of the cruel must fall also upon all who go out intentionally to kill God's creatures and call it "sport."

Such things as these you would not do, I know, and for the sake of the love of God, when opportunity offers, you will speak clearly against them. But there is a cruelty in speech as well as in act, and anyone who says a word with the intention to wound another is guilty of this crime. That, too, you would not do, but sometimes a careless word does as much harm as a malicious one. So you must be on your guard against unintentional cruelty.

It comes usually from thoughtlessness. Some people are so filled with greed and avarice that they never even think of the suffering that they cause to others by paying too little, or by half-starving their wives and children. Other people think only of their own lust and care little how many souls and bodies they ruin in satisfying it. Just to save themselves a few minutes' trouble, some employers do not pay their workmen on the proper day, thinking nothing of the difficulties they bring upon them. So much suffering is caused just by carelessness—by forgetting to think how an action will affect others. But karma never forgets, and it takes no account of the fact that people forget. If you wish to enter the path, you must think of the consequences of what you do, lest you should be guilty of thoughtless cruelty.

Superstition is another mighty evil, and has caused much terrible cruelty. The person who is a slave to it despises others who are wiser, tries to force them to do as he does. Think of the awful slaughter produced by the superstition that animals should be sacrificed and by the still more cruel superstition that we need flesh for food. Think of the treatment which superstition has meted out to the depressed classes in our beloved India, and see in that how this evil quality can breed heartless cruelty even among those who know the duty of brotherhood. Many crimes have been committed in the name of the God of love, because of this nightmare of superstition; be very careful therefore that not the slightest trace of it remains in you.

These three great crimes you must avoid, for they are fatal to all progress, because they sin against love. But not only must you thus refrain from evil, you must also be active in doing good. You must be so filled with the intense desire of service that you are ever on the watch to render it to all around you— not to human beings alone, but even to animals and plants. You must render it in small things every day, that the habit may be formed, so that you may not miss the rare opportunity when the great thing offers itself to be done. For if you yearn to be one with God, it is not for your own sake; it is that you may be a channel through which God's love may flow to reach your fellow human beings.

They who are on the path exist not for themselves, but for others; they have forgotten themselves, in order that they may serve others. They are a pen in the hand of God, through which God's thought may flow, and find for itself an expression down here, which without a pen it could not have. Yet at the same time they are also a living plume of fire, raying out upon the world the divine love that fills their hearts.

The wisdom which enables you to help, the will which directs the wisdom, the love which inspires the will—these are your qualifications. Will, wisdom, and love are the three aspects of the Logos; and you, who wish to enroll yourselves to serve God, must show forth these aspects in the world.

Waiting the word of the Master,
Watching the hidden light;
Listening to catch his orders
In the very midst of the fight;

Seeing his slightest signal
Across the heads of the throng;
Hearing his faintest whisper
Above earth's loudest song.

# Light on the Path

by Mabel Collins

# PREFACE

The first edition of this book was published in 1885, and on its title page it was described as "A treatise written for the personal use of those who are ignorant of the Eastern Wisdom and who desire to enter within its influence." The text itself is said to be of very ancient origin, written in an archaic form of Sanskrit. In its present form it was given through Mabel Collins, a member of the Theosophical Society in England, who at one time collaborated with H. P. Blavatsky in the editorship of the magazine *Lucifer*.

Since its first appearance in the last century, this little book has become a classic of Theosophical literature. It has been through dozens of editions in many languages.

The original verses are printed in heavy type. Amplifications of the original verses, together with commentaries, are printed in ordinary type. The essay on karma was also included in the first edition of the work.

— Editor

## PART ONE

These rules are written for all disciples:
Attend you to them.

Before the eyes can see they must be incapable of tears. Before the ear can hear, it must have lost its sensitiveness. Before the voice can speak in the presence of the Masters, it must have lost the power to wound. Before the soul can stand in the presence of the Masters, its feet must be washed in the blood of the heart.

### 1. Kill out ambition.

NOTE—Ambition is the first curse: the great tempter of the person who is rising above his fellows. It is the simplest form of looking for reward. People of intelligence and power are led away from their higher possibilities by it continually. Yet it is a necessary teacher. Its results turn to dust and ashes in the mouth; like death and estrangement, it shows us at last that to work for self is to work for disappointment. But though this first rule seems so simple and easy, do not quickly pass it by. For these vices of the ordinary person pass through a subtle transformation and reappear with changed aspect in the heart of the disciple. It is easy to say, "I will not be ambitious"; it is not so easy to say, "When the Master reads my heart, he will find it utterly clean." The pure artist who works for the love of the work is sometimes more firmly planted on the right road than esoteric students who fancy they have removed their interest from self, but who have in reality only enlarged the limits of experience and desire, and transferred their interest to things which concern their larger span of life. The same principle applies to the next two seemingly simple rules. Linger over them, and do not let yourself be easily deceived by your own heart. For now, at the threshold, a mistake can be corrected. But carry it with you and it will grow and come to fruition, or else you must suffer bitterly in its destruction.

**2. Kill out desire of life.**

**3. Kill out desire of comfort.**

4. Work as those work who are ambitious. Respect life as do those who desire it. Be happy as those are who live for happiness.

Seek in the heart the source of evil and expunge it. It lives fruitfully in the heart of the devoted disciple as well as in the heart of the person of desire. Only the strong can kill it out. The weak must wait for its growth, its fruition, its death. And it is a plant that lives and increases throughout the ages. It flowers when the individual has accumulated innumerable existences. Those who will enter upon the path of power must tear this thing out of their hearts. And then the heart will bleed, and the whole life of the person seem to be utterly dissolved. This ordeal must be endured: it may come at the first step of the perilous ladder that leads to the path of life; it may not come until the last. But, O disciple, remember that it has to be endured, and fasten the energies of your soul upon the task. Live neither in the present nor the future, but in the Eternal. This giant weed cannot flower there; this blot upon existence is wiped out by the very atmosphere of eternal thought.

### 5. Kill out all sense of separateness.

NOTE—Do not fancy you can stand aside from bad or foolish people. They are yourself, though in a lesser degree than your friend or your Master. But if you allow the idea of separateness from any evil thing or person to grow up within you, by so doing you create karma which will bind you to that thing or person till your soul recognizes that it cannot be isolated. Remember that the sin and shame of the world are your sin and shame, for you are a part of it; your karma is inextricably interwoven with the great karma. And before you can attain knowledge you must have passed through all places, foul and clean alike. Therefore, remember that the soiled garment you shrink from touching may have been yours yesterday, may be yours tomorrow. And if you turn with horror from it when it is flung upon your shoulders, it will cling the more closely to you. Self-righteous people make for themselves a bed of mire. Abstain because it is right to abstain—not that yourself shall be kept clean.

**6.** Kill out desire for sensation.

**7.** Kill out the hunger for growth.

8. Yet stand alone and isolated, because nothing that is embodied, nothing that is conscious of separation, nothing that is out of the Eternal, can aid you. Learn from sensation and observe it, because only so can you commence the science of self-knowledge, and plant your foot on the first step of the ladder. Grow as the flower grows, unconsciously, but eagerly anxious to open its soul to the air. So must you press forward to open your soul to the Eternal. But it must be the Eternal that draws forth your strength and beauty, not desire for growth. For in the one case you develop in the luxuriance of purity; in the other you harden by the forcible passion for personal stature.

**9.** Desire only that which is within you.

**10.** Desire only that which is beyond you.

**11.** Desire only that which is unattainable.

12. For within you is the light of the world—the only light that can be shed upon the path. If you are unable to perceive it within you, it is useless to look for it elsewhere. It is beyond you, because when you reach it you have lost yourself. It is unattainable, because it forever recedes. You will enter the light, but you will never touch the Flame.

**13.** Desire power ardently.

**14.** Desire peace fervently.

**15.** Desire possessions above all.

16. But those possessions must belong to the pure soul only, and be possessed therefore by all pure souls equally, and thus be the special property of the whole only when united. Hunger for such possessions as can be held by the pure soul, that you may accumulate wealth for that united spirit of life which is your only true Self. The peace you shall desire is that sacred peace which nothing can disturb, and in which the soul grows as does the holy flower upon the still lagoons. And that power which the disciples shall covet is that which shall make them appear as nothing in the eyes of others.

**17.** Seek out the way.

NOTE—These four words seem, perhaps, too slight to stand alone. The disciple may say, "Should I study these thoughts at all, did I not seek out the way?" Yet do not pass on hastily. Pause and consider awhile. Is it the way you desire, or is it that there is a dim perspective in your visions of great heights to be scaled by yourself, of a great future for you to compass? Be warned. The way is to be sought for its own sake, not with regard to your feet that shall tread it.

There is a correspondence between this rule and the seventeenth of the second series. When after ages of struggle and many victories the final battle is won, the final secret demanded, then you are prepared for a further path. When the final secret of this great lesson is told, in it is opened the mystery of the new way—a path which leads out of all human experience and which is utterly beyond human perception or imagination. At each of these points it is needful to pause long and consider well. At each of these points it is necessary to be sure that the way is chosen for its own sake. The way and the truth come first, then follows the life.

### 18. Seek the way by retreating within.

### 19. Seek the way by advancing boldly without.

20. Seek it not by any one road. To each temperament there is one road which seems the most desirable. But the way is not found by devotion alone, by religious contemplation alone, by ardent progress, by self-sacrificing labor, by studious observation of life. None alone can take the disciple more than one step onward. All steps are necessary to make up the ladder. Your vices become steps in the ladder, one by one, as they are surmounted. Your virtues are steps indeed, necessary—not by any means to be dispensed with. Yet, though they create a fair atmosphere and a happy future, they are useless if they stand alone. Our whole nature must be used wisely if we desire to enter the way. We are each to ourselves absolutely the way, the truth, and the life. But we are only so when we grasp our whole individuality firmly, and by the force of our awakened spiritual will, recognize this individuality as not ourselves, but rather that thing which we have with pain created for our own use and by means of which we purpose, as our growth slowly develops our intelligence, to reach to the life beyond individuality.

When we know that for this our wonderful complex separated life exists, then, indeed, and then only, are we upon the way. Seek it by plunging into the mysterious and glorious depths of your own inmost being. Seek it by testing all experience, by using the senses to understand the growth and meaning of individuality, and the beauty and obscurity of those other divine fragments which are struggling side by side with you. Seek it by studying the laws of being, the laws of Nature, the laws of the supernatural; and seek it by making the profound obeisance of the soul to the dim star that burns within. Steadily, as you watch and worship, its light will grow stronger. Then you may know you have found the beginning of the way. And when you have found the end, its light will suddenly become the infinite light.

NOTE—Seek it by testing all experience; and remember that when I say this I do not say: "Yield to the seduction of sense in order to know it." Before you have become an esoteric student you may do this—but not afterwards. When you have chosen and entered the path you cannot yield to these seductions without shame. Yet you can experience them without horror; can weigh, observe, and test them; and wait with the patience of confidence for the hour when they shall affect you no longer. But do not condemn those who yield; stretch out your hand to them as fellow pilgrims whose feet have become heavy with mire. Remember, O disciple, that great though the gulf may be between the good person and the sinner, it is greater between the good person and the one who has attained knowledge; it is immeasurable between the good person and one on the threshold of divinity. Therefore be wary lest too soon you fancy yourself a thing apart from the mass. When you have found the beginning of the way, the star of your soul will show its light, and by that light you will perceive how great is the darkness in which it burns. Mind, heart, brain all are obscure and dark until the first great battle has been won. Do not be appalled and terrified by the sight; keep your eyes fixed on the small light and it will grow. But let the darkness within help you to understand the helplessness of those who have seen no light, whose souls are in profound gloom. Blame them not. Shrink not from them, but try to lift a little of the heavy karma of the world; give your aid to the few strong hands that hold back the powers of darkness from obtaining complete victory. Then do you enter into a partnership of joy, which brings indeed terrible toil and profound sadness, but also a great and ever-increasing delight.

21. Look for the flower to bloom in the silence that follows the storm: not till then.

It shall grow; it will shoot up; it will make branches and leaves and form buds, while the storm continues, while the battle lasts. But not till the whole human personality is dissolved and melted— not until it is held by the divine fragment which has created it, as a mere subject for grave experiment and experience—not until the whole nature has yielded and become subject to its higher Self, can the bloom open. Then will come a calm such as comes in a tropical country after the heavy rain, when Nature works so swiftly that one may see her action. Such a calm will come to the harassed spirit. And in the deep silence the mysterious event will occur which will prove that the way has been found. Call it by what name you will, it is a voice that speaks where there is none to speak—it is a messenger that comes, a messenger without form or substance; or it is the flower of the soul that has opened. It cannot be described by any metaphor. But it can be felt after, looked for, and desired, even amid the raging of the storm. The silence may last a moment of time or it may last a thousand years. But it will end. Yet you will carry its strength with you. Again and again the battle must be fought and won. It is only for an interval that Nature can be still.

NOTE—The opening of the bloom is the glorious moment when perception awakes; with it comes confidence, knowledge, certainty. The pause of the soul is the moment of wonder, and the next moment of satisfaction—that is the silence.

Know, O disciple, that those who have passed through the silence, and felt its peace and retained its strength, they long that you shall pass through it also. Therefore, in the Hall of Learning, when you are capable of entering there, you will always find your Master.

Those that ask shall have. But though ordinary people ask perpetually, their voices are not heard. For they ask with the mind only, and the voice of the mind is only heard on that plane on which the mind acts. Therefore not until the first twenty-one rules are passed do I say that those that ask shall have.

To read, in the inner sense, is to read with the eyes of the spirit. To ask is to feel the hunger within— the yearning of spiritual aspiration. To be able to read means having obtained the power in a small degree of satisfying that hunger. When disciples are ready to learn, then they are accepted, acknowledged, recognized. It must be so, for they have lit their lamp, and it cannot be hidden. But to learn is impossible until the first great battle has been won. The mind may recognize truth, but the spirit cannot receive it. Once having passed through the storm and attained the peace, it is then always possible to learn, even though the disciples waver, hesitate, and turn aside. The Voice of the Silence remains within them, and though they leave the path utterly, yet one day it will resound, rend them asunder, and separate their passions from their divine possibilities. Then, with pain and desperate cries from the deserted lower self, they will return.

Therefore I say, Peace be with you. "My peace I give unto you" can only be said by the Master to the beloved disciples who are as himself. There are some, even among those who are unaware of the Eastern Wisdom, to whom this can be said, and to whom it can daily be said with more completeness.

Regard the three truths. They are equal.

These written above are the first of the rules which are written on the walls of the Hall of Learning. Those that ask shall have. Those that desire to read shall read. Those who desire to learn shall learn.

## PEACE BE WITH YOU

Three truths of the White Lotus
from the eighth chapter of *The Idyll of the White Lotus*

There are Three Truths which are absolute and cannot be lost, but yet may remain silent for lack of speech.

1. The human soul is immortal, and its future is the future of a thing whose growth and splendor has no limit.

2. The principle which gives life dwells in us, and around us, is undying and eternally beneficent, is not heard, or seen, or smelt, but is perceived by the one who desires perception.

3. We are each our own absolute lawgiver, the dispenser of glory or gloom to ourselves; the decreer of our life, our reward, our punishment.

These Truths, which are as great as is life itself, are as simple as the simplest human mind. Feed the hungry with them.

## PART TWO

Out of the silence that is peace a resonant voice shall arise. And this voice will say: It is not well; thou hast reaped, now thou must sow. And knowing this voice to be the silence itself you will obey.

You who are now a disciple—able to stand, able to hear, able to see, able to speak—who have conquered desire and attained to self-knowledge, who have seen your soul in its bloom and recognized it, and heard the Voice of the Silence—go to the Hall of Learning and read what is written there for you.

NOTE—To be able to stand is to have confidence; to be able to hear is to have opened the doors of the soul; to be able to see is to have attained perception; to be able to speak is to have attained the power of helping others; to have conquered desire is to have learned how to use and control the self; to have attained to self-knowledge is to have retreated to the inner fortress where the personal self can be viewed with impartiality; to have seen your soul in its bloom is to have obtained a momentary glimpse in yourself of the transfiguration which will eventually make you more than human; to recognize is to achieve the great task of gazing upon the blazing light without dropping the eyes or falling back in terror, as though before some ghastly phantom. This happens to some, and so when the victory is all but won it is lost.

To hear the Voice of the Silence is to understand that from within comes the only true guidance; to go to the Hall of Learning is to enter the state in which learning becomes possible. Then will many words be written there for you, and written in fiery letters for you to read easily. For when the disciple is ready the Master is ready also.

**1. Stand aside in the coming battle, and though thou fightest be not thou the warrior.**

**2. Look for the Warrior and let him fight in thee.**

**3. Take his orders for battle and obey them.**

4. Obey him, not as though he were a general, but as though he were yourself, and his spoken words were the utterance of your secret desires; for he is yourself, yet infinitely wiser and stronger than yourself. Look for him, else in the fever and hurry of the fight you may pass him, and he will not know you unless you know him. If your cry reaches his listening ear, then he will fight in you and fill the dull void within. And if this is so, then you can go through the fight cool and unwearied, standing aside and letting him battle for you. Then it will be impossible for you to strike one blow amiss. But if you do not look for him, if you pass him by, then there is no safeguard

for you. Your brain will reel, your heart grow uncertain, and in the dust of the battlefield your sight and senses will fail, and you will not know your friends from your enemies.

He is yourself, yet you are but finite and liable to error. He is eternal and is sure. He is eternal truth. When once he has entered you and become your Warrior, he will never utterly desert you, and at the day of the great peace he will become one with you.

## 5. Listen to the song of life.

NOTE—Look for it and listen to it first in your own heart. At first you may say: "It is not there; when I search I find only discord." Look deeper. If again you are disappointed, pause and look deeper again. There is a natural melody, an obscure fount in every human heart. It may be hidden and utterly concealed and silenced—but it is there. At the very base of your nature you will find faith, hope, and love. Those that choose evil refuse to look within themselves, shut their ears to the melody of their hearts, as they blind their eyes to the light of their souls. They do this because they find it easier to live in desires. But underneath all life is the strong current that cannot be checked; the great waters are there in reality. Find them and you will perceive that all, even the most wretched of creatures, are a part of it, however they blind themselves to the fact and build up for themselves a phantasmal outer form of horror. In that sense it is that I say to you: all those beings among whom you struggle on are fragments of the Divine. And so deceptive is the illusion in which you live, that it is hard to guess where you will first detect the sweet voice in the hearts of others. But know that it is certainly within yourself. Look for it there and once having heard it, you will more readily recognize it around you.

**6. Store in your memory the melody you hear.**

**7. Learn from it the lesson of harmony.**

8. You can stand upright now, firm as a rock amid the turmoil, obeying the Warrior who is yourself and your king. Unconcerned in the battle save to do his bidding, having no longer any care as to the result of the battle, for one thing only is important, that the Warrior shall win, and you know he is incapable of defeat—standing thus, cool and awakened, use the hearing you have acquired by pain and by the destruction of pain. Only fragments of the great song come to your ears while you are but human. But if you listen to it, remember it faithfully, so that no fragment which has reached you is lost, and endeavor to learn from it the meaning of the mystery which surrounds you. In time you will need no teacher. For as the individual has voice, so has that in which the individual exists. Life itself has speech and is never silent. And its utterance is not, as you that are deaf may suppose, a cry; it is a song. Learn from it that you are part of the harmony; learn from it to obey the laws of the harmony.

**9. Regard earnestly all the life that surrounds you.**

**10.** **Learn to look intelligently into the hearts of men.**

NOTE—Look from an absolutely impersonal point of view, otherwise your sight is colored. Therefore impersonality must be first understood.

Intelligence is impartial: no one is your enemy; no one is your friend. All alike are your teachers. Your enemy becomes a mystery that must be solved, even though it takes ages, for human nature must be understood. Your friend becomes a part of yourself, an extension of yourself, a riddle hard to read. Only one thing is more difficult to know—your own heart. Not until the bonds of personality are loosed can that profound mystery of self begin to be seen. Not till you stand aside from it, will it in any way reveal itself to your understanding. Then, and not till then, can you grasp and guide it. Then, and not till then, can you use all its powers and devote them to a worthy service.

**11.** **Regard most earnestly your own heart.**

12. For through your own heart comes the one light which can illuminate life and make it clear to your eyes.

Study the hearts of others, that you may know what is that world in which you live and of which you will to be a part. Regard the constantly changing and moving life which surrounds you, for it is formed by human hearts; and as you learn to understand their constitution and meaning, you will by degrees be able to read the larger word of life.

13. Speech comes only with knowledge. Attain to knowledge and you will attain to speech.

NOTE—It is impossible to help others till you have obtained some certainty of your own. When you have learned the first twenty-one rules and have entered the Hall of Learning with your powers developed and senses unchained, then you will find there is a fount within you from which speech will arise.

After the thirteenth rule I can add no words to what is already written.

My peace I give unto you.

These notes are written only for those to whom I give my peace; those who can read what I have written with the inner as well as the outer sense.

14. Having obtained the use of the inner senses, having conquered the desires of the outer senses, having conquered the desires of the individual soul, and having obtained knowledge, prepare now, O disciple, to enter upon the way in reality. The path is found; make yourself ready to tread it.

15. Inquire of the earth, the air, and the water of the secrets they hold for you.

The development of your inner senses will enable you to do this.

**16.** **Inquire of the Holy Ones of the earth of the secrets they hold for you.**

The conquering of the desires of the outer senses will give you the right to this.

**17.** **Inquire of the inmost, the One, of its final secret, which it holds for you through the ages.**

The great and difficult victory, the conquering of the desires of the individual soul, is a work of ages; therefore do not expect to obtain its reward until ages of experience have been accumulated. When the time of learning this seventeenth rule is reached, the human is on the threshold of becoming more than human.

18. The knowledge which is now yours is only yours because your soul has become one with all pure souls and with the inmost. It is a trust vested in you by the Most High. Betray it, misuse your knowledge, or neglect it, and it is possible even now for you to fall from the high estate you have attained. Great ones fall back, even from the threshold, unable to sustain the weight of their responsibility, unable to pass on. Therefore look forward always with awe and trembling to this moment, and be prepared for the battle.

It is written that for one who is on the threshold of divinity no law can be framed, no guide can exist. Yet to enlighten the disciple, the final struggle may be thus expressed:

*19.* Hold fast to that which has neither sub-stance nor existence.

*20.* Listen only to the voice which is sound-less.

*21.* Look only on that which is invisible alike to the inner and the outer sense.

### PEACE BE WITH YOU

# KARMA

Consider with me that the individual existence is a rope which stretches from the infinite to the infinite, and has no end and no commencement, neither is it capable of being broken. This rope is formed of innumerable fine threads, which, lying closely together, form its thickness. These threads are colorless, are perfect in their qualities of straightness, strength, and levelness. This rope, passing as it does through all places, suffers strange accidents. Very often a thread is caught and becomes attached, or perhaps is only violently pulled from its even way. Then for a long time it is disordered and it disorders the whole. Sometimes one is stained with dirt or with color, and not only does the stain run on further than the spot of contact, but it discolors other threads. And remember that the threads are living—are like electric wires; more, are like quivering nerves. How far then must the stain, the drag awry, be communicated! But eventually the long strands, the living threads which in their unbroken continuity form the individual, pass out of the shadow into the shine. Then the threads are no longer colorless, but golden; once more they lie

59

together level. Once more harmony is established between them; and from that harmony within, the greater harmony is perceived.

This illustration presents but a small portion—a single side of the truth; it is less than a fragment. Yet, dwell on it; by its aid you may be led to perceive more. What is necessary to understand first is, not that the future is arbitrarily formed by any separate acts of the present, but that the whole of the future is in unbroken continuity with the present, as the present is with the past. On one plane, from one point of view, the illustration of the rope is correct.

It is said that a little attention to esoteric teachings produces great karmic results. That is because it is impossible to give any attention to the ancient wisdom without making a definite choice between what are familiarly called good and evil. The first step in esoteric study brings the student to the tree of knowledge. You must pluck and eat; you must choose. No longer are you capable of the indecision of ignorance. You go on, either on the good or on the evil path. And to step definitely and knowingly even one step on either path produces great karmic results. The mass of humanity walk waveringly, uncertain as to the goal they aim at; their standard of life is indefinite; consequently their karma operates in a confused manner. But when once the threshold of knowledge is reached, the confusion begins to lessen, and consequently the karmic results increase enormously, because all are acting in the same direction on all

the different planes; for students of esoteric knowledge cannot be halfhearted, nor can they return when
they have passed the threshold. These things are as
impossible as that the adult should become the child
again. The individuality has approached the state of
responsibility by reason of growth; it cannot recede
from it.

Those who would escape from the bondage of
karma must raise their individuality out of the shadow
into the shine; must so elevate their existence that
these threads do not come in contact with soiling
substances, do not become so attached as to be pulled
away. They simply lift themselves out of the region
in which karma operates. They do not leave the existence which they are experiencing because of that.
The ground may be rough and dirty, or full of rich
flowers whose pollen stains, and of sweet substances
that cling and become attachments—but overhead
there is always the free sky. Those who desire to be
karma-less must look to the air for home; and after
that to the ether. Those who desire to form good
karma will meet with many confusions, and in the
effort to sow rich seed for their own harvesting may
plant a thousand weeds, and among them the giant.
Desire to sow no seed for your own harvesting; desire
only to sow that seed the fruit of which shall feed
the world. You are a part of the world; in giving it food
you feed yourself. Yet in even this thought there lurks
a great danger which starts forward and faces disciples
who have long thought themselves working for good,
while in their inmost souls they have perceived only

evil; that is, they have thought themselves to be intending great benefit to the world, while all the time they have unconsciously embraced the thought of karma; and the great benefits they work for are for themselves. They may refuse to allow themselves to think of reward. But in that very refusal is seen the fact that reward is desired. And it is useless for disciples to srive to learn by means of checking themselves. The soul must be unfettered, the desires free. But until they are fixed on that state wherein there is neither reward nor punishment, good nor evil, it is in vain that they endeavor. They may seem to make great progress, but some day they will come face to face with their own souls, and will recognize that when they came to the tree of knowledge they chose the bitter fruit and not the sweet; and then the veil will fall utterly, and they will give up their freedom and become slaves of desire. Therefore be warned, you who are but turning towards the life of the ancient wisdom. Learn now that there is no cure for desire, no cure for the love of reward, no cure for the misery of longing, save in the fixing of the sight and hearing upon that which is invisible and soundless. Begin even now to practice it, and so a thousand serpents will be kept from your path. Live in the eternal.

The operations of the actual laws of karma are not to be studied until the disciple has reached the point at which they no longer affect the disciple. Initiates have a right to demand the secrets of Nature and to know the rules which govern human life. They obtain this right by having escaped the limits of

Nature and by having freed themselves from the rules which govern human life. They have become recognized portions of the divine element and are no longer affected by that which is temporary. They then obtain the knowledge of the laws which govern temporary conditions. Therefore you who desire to understand the laws of karma, attempt first to free yourself from these laws; and this can only be done by fixing your attention on that which is unaffected by those laws.

# The Voice
## of the Silence
by H. P. Blavatsky

# PREFACE

The following pages are derived from *The Book of the Golden Precepts*, one of the works put into the hands of mystic students in the East. The knowledge of them is obligatory in that school, the teachings of which are accepted by many Theosophists. Therefore, as I know many of these precepts by heart, the work of translating has been a relatively easy task for me.

It is well known that in India the methods of psychic development differ with the gurus (teachers or masters), not only because of their belonging to different schools of philosophy, of which there are six, but because every guru has his own system, which he generally keeps very secret. But beyond the Himalayas the method in the esoteric schools does not differ, unless the guru is simply a lama, but little more learned than those he teaches.

The work from which I here translate forms part of the same series as that from which the Stanzas of the *Book of Dzyan* were taken, on which *The Secret Doctrine* is based. Together with the great mystic work

called *Paramartha*, which, the legend of Nagarjuna
tells us, was delivered to the great arhat by the *Nagas*
or "serpents" (in truth a name given to the ancient
Initiates), *The Book of the Golden Precepts* claims the
same origin. Yet its maxims and ideas, however noble
and original, are often found under different forms in
Sanskrit works, such as the *Jnaneshvari*, that superb
mystic treatise in which Krishna describes to Arjuna
in glowing colors the condition of a fully illumined
Yogi, and again in certain Upanishads. This is but
natural, since most if not all of the greatest arhats, the
first followers of Gautama Buddha, were Hindus and
Aryans, not Mongolians, especially those who emi-
grated into Tibet. The works left by Aryasanga alone
are very numerous.

The original *Precepts* are engraved on thin ob-
long squares, copies very often on discs. These discs
or plates are generally preserved on the altars of
the temples attached to centers where the so-called
contemplative or Mahayana (Yogachara) schools are
established. They are written variously, sometimes in
Tibetan but mostly in ideographs. The sacerdotal language (Senzar), besides an alphabet of its own, may be
rendered in several modes of writing in cipher characters, which partake more of the nature of ideographs
than of syllables. Another method (*lug,* in Tibetan) is
to use the numerals and colors, each of which corre-
spond to a letter of the Tibetan alphabet (thirty simple and seventy-four compound letters) thus forming
a complete cryptographic alphabet. When the ideographs are used there is a definite mode of reading

the text, as in this case the symbols and signs used in astrology, namely the twelve zodiacal animals and the seven primary colors—each a triplet in shade, i.e., the light, the primary, and the dark—stand for the thirty-three letters of the simple alphabet, for words and sentences. For in this method, the twelve "animals" five times repeated and coupled with the five elements and the seven colors, furnish a whole alphabet composed of sixty sacred letters and twelve signs. A sign placed at the beginning of the text determines whether the reader has to spell it according to the Indian mode, when every word is simply a Sanskrit adaptation, or according to the Chinese principle of reading the ideographs. The easiest way, however, is that which allows the reader to use no special, or *any* language he likes, as the signs and symbols were, like the Arabic numerals or figures, common and international property among initiated mystics and their followers. The same peculiarity is characteristic of one of the Chinese modes of writing, which can be read with equal facility by anyone acquainted with the character: for instance, the Japanese can read it in their own language as readily as the Chinese in theirs.

*The Book of the Golden Precepts*—some of which are pre-Buddhistic while others belong to a later date—contains about ninety distinct little treatises. Of these I learned thirty-nine by heart, years ago. To translate the rest, I should have to resort to notes scattered among a too large number of papers and memoranda collected for the last twenty years and

never put in order, to make of it by any means an
easy task. Nor could they be all translated and given
to a world too selfish and too much attached to
objects of sense to be in any way prepared to receive
such exalted ethics in the right spirit. For, unless a
man perseveres seriously in the pursuit of self-knowledge, he will never lend a willing ear to advice of
this nature.

And yet such ethics fill volumes upon volumes
in Eastern literature, especially in the Upanishads.
"Kill out all desire of life," says Krishna to Arjuna.
That desire lingers only in the body, the vehicle of
the embodied self, not in the Self which is "eternal,
indestructible, which kills not nor is it killed" (*Katha
Upanishad*). "Kill out sensation," teaches *Sutta Nipata*,
"look alike on pleasure and pain, gain and loss, victory and defeat." Again, "Seek shelter in the eternal
alone" (ibid.). "Destroy the sense of separateness," re-
peats Krishna under every form. "The mind (*manas*)
which follows the rambling senses, makes the soul
(*buddhi*) as helpless as the boat which the wind leads
astray upon the waters" (Bhagavad Gita II. 70).

Therefore it has been thought better to make
a judicious selection only from those treatises which
will best suit the few real mystics in the Theosophical
Society and which are sure to answer their needs. It is
only these who will appreciate the words of Krishna-
Christos, the Higher Self:

"Sages do not grieve for the living nor the dead.
Never did I not exist, nor you, nor these rulers of men;

nor will any one of us ever hereafter cease to be" (Bhagavad Gita II. 27).

In this translation, I have done my best to preserve the poetical beauty of language and imagery which characterize the original. How far this effort has been successful is for the reader to judge.

—H.P.B.

Dedicated to the Few

# FRAGMENT ONE
## The Voice of the Silence

1. These instructions are for those ignorant of the dangers of the lower *iddhi*.[1]

2. He who would hear the voice of *nada*,[2] "the Soundless Sound," and comprehend it, he has to learn the nature of *Dharana*.[3]

3. Having become indifferent to objects of perception, the pupil must seek out the *raja* of the senses, the thought producer, he who awakes illusion.

4. The mind is the great slayer of the Real.

5. Let the disciple slay the slayer.

For:

6. When to himself his form appears unreal, as do on waking all the forms he sees in dreams;

7. When he has ceased to hear the many, he may discern the ONE—the inner sound which kills the outer.

8. Then only, not till then, shall he forsake the region of *asat*, the false, to come unto the realm of *Sat*, the true.

9. Before the soul can see, the harmony within must be attained, and fleshly eyes be rendered blind to all illusion.

10. Before the soul can hear, the image (man) has to become as deaf to roarings as to whispers, to cries of bellowing elephants as to the silvery buzzing of the golden firefly.

11. Before the soul can comprehend and may remember, she must unto the Silent Speaker be united, just as the form to which the clay is modeled, is first united with the potter's mind.

12. For then the soul will hear, and will remember.

13. And then to the inner ear will speak

THE VOICE OF THE SILENCE

And say:

14. If thy soul smiles while bathing in the sunlight of thy life; if thy soul sings within her chrysalis of flesh and matter; if thy soul weeps inside her castle of illusion; if thy soul struggles to break the silver thread that binds her to the Master;[4] know, O disciple, thy soul is of the earth.

15. When to the world's turmoil thy budding soul[5] lends ear; when to the roaring voice of the great

illusion thy soul responds;[6] when frightened at the sight of the hot tears of pain, when deafened by the cries of distress, thy soul withdraws like the shy turtle within the carapace of selfhood, learn, O disciple, of her silent God, thy soul is an unworthy shrine.

16. When waxing stronger, thy soul glides forth from her secure retreat, and breaking loose from the protecting shrine, extends her silver thread and rushes onward; when beholding her image on the waves of space she whispers, "This is I,"—declare, O disciple, that thy soul is caught in the webs of delusion.[7]

17. This earth, disciple, is the Hall of Sorrow, wherein are set along the path of dire probations, traps to ensnare thy Ego by the delusion called Great Heresy.[8]

18. This earth, O ignorant disciple, is but the dismal entrance leading to the twilight that precedes the valley of true light—that light which no wind can extinguish, that light which burns without a wick or fuel.

19. Saith the Great Law: "In order to become the Knower of All Self,[9] thou hast first of Self to be the knower." To reach the knowledge of that Self thou has to give up self to non-self, being to non-being, and then thou canst repose between the wings of the Great Bird. Aye, sweet is rest between the wings of that which is not born, nor dies, but is the AUM[10] throughout eternal ages.[11]

20. Bestride the Bird of Life, if thou wouldst know.[12]

21. Give up thy life, if thou wouldst live.[13]

22. Three halls, O weary pilgrim, lead to the end of toils. Three halls, O conqueror of Mara, will bring thee through three states[14] into the fourth[15] and thence into the seven worlds,[16] the worlds of rest eternal.

23. If thou wouldst learn their names, then hearken, and remember.

24. The name of the first hall is Ignorance— *Avidya*.

25. It is the hall in which thou saw'st the light, in which thou livest and shalt die.[17]

26. The name of hall the second is the Hall of Learning [the Hall of *Probationary* Learning]. In it thy soul will find the blossoms of life, but under every flower a serpent coiled.[18]

27. The name of the third hall is Wisdom, beyond which stretch the shoreless waters of Akshara, the indestructible fount of omniscience.[19]

28. If thou wouldst cross the first hall safely, let not thy mind mistake the fires of lust that burn therein for the sunlight of life.

29. If thou wouldst cross the second safely, stop not the fragrance of its stupefying blossoms to inhale. If freed thou wouldst be from the karmic chains, seek not for thy guru in those mayavic regions.

30. The wise ones tarry not in pleasure grounds of senses.

31. The wise ones heed not the sweet-tongued voices of illusion.

32. Seek for him who is to give thee birth,[20] in the Hall of Wisdom, the hall which lies beyond, wherein all shadows are unknown, and where the light of truth shines with unfading glory.

33. That which is uncreate abides in thee, disciple, as it abides in that hall. If thou wouldst reach it and blend the two, thou must divest thyself of thy dark garments of illusion. Stifle the voice of flesh, allow no image of the senses to get between its light and thine that thus the twain may blend in one. And having learnt thine own *ajnana*,[21] flee from the Hall of Learning. This hall is dangerous in its perfidious beauty, is needed but for thy probation. Beware, lanoo, lest dazzled by illusive radiance thy soul should linger and be caught in its deceptive light.

34. This light shines from the jewel of the great ensnarer (Mara).[22] The senses it bewitches, blinds the mind, and leaves the unwary an abandoned wreck.

35. The moth attracted to the dazzling flame of thy night lamp is doomed to perish in the viscid oil. The unwary soul that fails to grapple with the mocking demon of illusion, will return to earth the slave of Mara.

36. Behold the hosts of souls. Watch how they hover o'er the stormy sea of human life, and how

exhausted, bleeding, broken-winged, they drop one after other on the swelling waves. Tossed by the fierce winds, chased by the gale, they drift into the eddies and disappear within the first great vortex.

37. If through the Hall of Wisdom, thou wouldst reach the Vale of Bliss, disciple, close fast thy senses against the great dire heresy of separateness that weans thee from the rest.

38. Let not thy "Heaven-born," merged in the sea of Maya, break from the Universal Parent (Soul), but let the fiery power retire into the inmost chamber, the chamber of the Heart[23] and the abode of the World's Mother.[24]

39. Then from the heart that power shall rise into the sixth, the middle region, the place between thine eyes, when it becomes the breath of the ONE-SOUL, the voice which filleth all, thy Master's voice.

40. 'Tis only then thou canst become a "Walker of the Sky"[25] who treads the winds above the waves, whose step touches not the waters.

41. Before thou settest thy foot upon the ladder's upper rung, the ladder of the mystic sounds, thou hast to hear the voice of thy *inner* God [the Higher Self] in seven manners.

42. The first is like the nightingale's sweet voice chanting a song of parting to its mate.

43. The second comes as the sound of a silver cymbal of the Dhyanis, awakening the twinkling stars.

44. The next is as the plaint melodious of the ocean sprite imprisoned in its shell.

45. And this is followed by the chant of vina.[26]

46. The fifth like sound of bamboo flute shrills in thine ear.

47. It changes next into a trumpet blast.

48. The last vibrates like the dull rumbling of a thundercloud.

49. The seventh swallows all the other sounds. They die, and then are heard no more.

50. When the six[27] are slain and at the Master's feet are laid, then is the pupil merged into the ONE,[28] becomes that One and lives therein.

51. Before that path is entered, thou must destroy thy lunar body,[29] cleanse thy mind-body[30] and make clean thy heart.

52. Eternal life's pure waters, clear and crystal, with the monsoon tempest's muddy torrents cannot mingle.

53. Heaven's dewdrop glittering in the morn's first sunbeam within the bosom of the lotus, when dropped on earth becomes a piece of clay; behold, the pearl is now a speck of mire.

54. Strive with thy thoughts unclean before they overpower thee. Use them as they will thee, for if thou sparest them and they take root and grow, know well, these thoughts will overpower and kill

thee. Beware, disciple, suffer not, even though it be their shadow, to approach. For it will grow, increase in size and power, and then this thing of darkness will absorb thy being before thou hast well realized the black foul monster's presence.

55. Before the mystic power [Kundalini][31] can make of thee a god, lanoo, thou must have gained the faculty to slay thy lunar form at will.

56. The self of matter and the Self of Spirit can never meet. One of the twain must disappear; there is no place for both.

57. Ere thy Soul's mind can understand, the bud of personality must be crushed out, the worm of sense destroyed past resurrection.

58. Thou canst not travel on the Path before thou has become that path itself.[32]

59. Let thy soul lend its ear to every cry of pain like as the lotus bares its heart to drink the morning sun.

60. Let not the fierce sun dry one tear of pain before thyself hast wiped it from the sufferer's eye.

61. But let each burning human tear drop on thy heart and there remain, nor ever brush it off, until the pain that caused it is removed.

62. These tears, O thou of heart most merciful, these are the streams that irrigate the fields of charity immortal. 'Tis on such soil that grows the midnight blossom of Buddha[33] more difficult to find, more rare

to view than is the flower of the vogay tree. It is the seed of freedom from rebirth. It isolates the Arhat both from strife and lust; it leads him through the fields of being unto the peace and bliss known only in the land of silence and non-being.

63. Kill out desire; but if thou killest it take heed lest from the dead it should again arise.

64. Kill love of life; but if thou slayest *tanha*,[34] let this not be for thirst of life eternal, but to replace the fleeting by the everlasting.

65. Desire nothing. Chafe not at karma, nor at nature's changeless laws. But struggle only with the personal, the transitory, the evanescent, and the perishable.

66. Help Nature and work on with her; and Nature will regard thee as one of her creators and make obeisance.

67. And she will open wide before thee the portals of her secret chambers, lay bare before thy gaze the treasures hidden in the very depths of her pure virgin bosom. Unsullied by the hand of matter, she shows her treasures only to the eye of Spirit—the eye which never closes, the eye for which there is no veil in all her kingdoms.

68. Then will she show thee the means and way, the first gate and the second, the third, up to the very seventh. And then, the goal—beyond which lie, bathed in the sunlight of the Spirit, glories untold, unseen by any save the eye of Soul.

69. There is but one road to the Path; at its very end alone the Voice of the Silence can be heard. The ladder by which the candidate ascends is formed of rungs of suffering and pain; these can be silenced only by the voice of virtue. Woe, then, to thee, disciple, if there is one single vice thou has not left behind. For then the ladder will give way and overthrow thee; its foot rests in the deep mire of thy sins and failings, and ere thou canst attempt to cross this wide abyss of matter thou has to lave thy feet in waters of renunciation. Beware lest thou shouldst set a foot still soiled upon the ladder's lowest rung. Woe unto him who dares pollute one rung with miry feet. The foul and viscous mud will dry, become tenacious, then glue his feet unto the spot, and like a bird caught in the wily fowler's lime, he will be stayed from further progress. His vices will take shape and drag him down. His sins will raise their voices like as the jackal's laugh and sob after the sun goes down; his thoughts become an army, and bear him off a captive slave.

70. Kill thy desires, lanoo, make thy vices impotent, ere the first step is taken on the solemn journey.

71. Strangle thy sins, and make them dumb forever, before thou dost lift one foot to mount the ladder.

72. Silence thy thoughts and fix thy whole attention on thy Master whom yet thou dost not see, but whom thou feelest.

73. Merge into one sense thy senses, if thou wouldst be secure against the foe. 'Tis by that sense

alone which lies concealed within the hollow of
thy brain, that the steep path which leadeth to thy
Master may be disclosed before thy soul's dim eyes.

74. Long and weary is the way before thee, O
disciple. One single thought about the past that thou
has left behind, will drag thee down and thou wilt
have to start the climb anew.

75. Kill in thyself all memory of past experiences. Look not behind or thou art lost.

76. Do not believe that lust can ever be killed
out if gratified or satiated, for this is an abomination
inspired by Mara. It is by feeding vice that it expands
and waxes strong, like to the worm that fattens on the
blossom's heart.

77. The rose must rebecome the bud born of
its parent stem, before the parasite has eaten through
its heart and drunk its life sap.

78. The golden tree puts forth its jewel buds
before its trunk is withered by the storm.

79. The pupil must regain the child-state he
has lost ere the first sound can fall upon his ear.

80. The light from the ONE Master, the one
unfading golden light of Spirit, shoots its effulgent
beams on the disciple from the very first. Its rays
thread through the thick dark clouds of matter.

81. Now here, now there, these rays illumine
it, like sun sparks light the earth through the thick
foliage of the jungle growth. But, O disciple, unless

the flesh is passive, head cool, the soul as firm and pure as flaming diamond, the radiance will not reach the chamber [see note 23, verse 38], its sunlight will not warm the heart, nor will the mystic sounds of the Akashic heights[35] reach the ear, however eager, at the initial stage.

82. Unless thou hearest, thou canst not see.

83. Unless thou seest, thou canst not hear. To hear and see, this is the second stage.

84. When the disciple sees and hears, and when he smells and tastes, eyes closed, ears shut, with mouth and nostrils stopped; when the four senses blend and are ready to pass into the fifth, that of the inner touch—then into stage the fourth he hath passed on.

85. And in the fifth, O slayer of thy thoughts, all these again have to be killed beyond reanimation.[36]

86. Withhold thy mind from all external objects, all external sights. Withhold internal images, lest on thy soul-light a dark shadow they should cast.

87. Thou art now in Dharana,[37] the sixth stage.

88. When thou hast passed into the seventh, O happy one, thou shalt perceive no more the sacred three,[38] for thou shalt have become that three thyself.

Thyself and mind, like twins upon a line, the star which is thy goal, burns overhead.[39] The three that dwell in glory and in bliss ineffable, now in the world of Maya have lost their names. They have become one star, the fire that burns but scorches not, that fire which is the upadhi[40] of the Flame.

89. And this, O yogi of success, is what men call Dhyana,[41] the right precursor of Samadhi.[42]

90. And now thy self is lost in Self, thyself unto Thyself, merged in that Self from which thou first didst radiate.

91. Where is thy individuality, lanoo, where the lanoo himself? It is the spark lost in the fire, the drop within the ocean, the ever-present ray become the All and the eternal radiance.

92. And now, lanoo, thou art the doer and the witness, the radiator and the radiation, light in the sound, and the sound in the light.

93. Thou art acquainted with the five impediments, O blessed one. Thou art their conqueror, the master of the sixth, deliverer of the four modes of truth.[43] The light that falls upon them shines from thyself, O thou who wast disciple, but art teacher now.

And of these modes of truth:

94. Hast thou not passed through knowledge of all misery—truth the first?

95. Hast thou not conquered the Maras' King at Tsi, the portal of assembling—truth the second?[44]

96. Hast thou not sin at the third gate destroyed and truth the third attained?

97. Has not thou entered *Tao*, the path that leads to knowledge—the fourth truth?[45]

98. And now, rest beneath the Bodhi tree, which is perfection of all knowledge, for, know, thou art the Master of Samadhi—the state of faultless vision.

99. Behold! thou hast become the light, thou hast become the sound, thou art thy Master and thy God. Thou art Thyself the object of thy search: the VOICE unbroken, that resounds throughout eternities, exempt from change, from sin exempt, the seven sounds in one,

THE VOICE OF THE SILENCE.

100. *Om Tat Sat*.

# FRAGMENT TWO
## The Two Paths

**101.** And now, O Teacher of Compassion, point thou the way to other men. Behold, all those who knocking for admission, await in ignorance and darkness to see the gate of the Sweet Law flung open!

The voice of the candidates:

**102.** Shalt not thou, Master of thine own mercy, reveal the Doctrine of the Heart?[46] Shalt thou refuse to lead thy servants unto the Path of Liberation?

Quoth the Teacher:

**103.** The Paths are two; the great Perfections three; six are the Virtues that transform the body into the Tree of Knowledge.[47]

**104.** Who shall approach them?

**105.** Who shall first enter them?

**106.** Who shall first hear the doctrine of two Paths in one, the truth unveiled about the Secret

Heart?[48] The Law which, shunning learning, teaches wisdom, reveals a tale of woe.

107. Alas, alas, that all men should possess Alaya, be one with the great Soul, and that possessing it, Alaya should so little avail them!

108. Behold how like the moon, reflected in the tranquil waves, Alaya is reflected by the small and by the great, is mirrored in the tiniest atoms, yet fails to reach the heart of all. Alas, that so few men should profit by the gift, the priceless boon of learning truth, the right perception of existing things, the knowledge of the nonexistent!

Saith the pupil:

109. O Teacher, what shall I do to reach to wisdom?

110. O Wise One, what, to gain perfection?

111. Search for the Paths. But, O lanoo, be of clean heart before thou startest on thy journey. Before thou takest thy first step learn to discern the real from the false, the ever-fleeting from the everlasting. Learn above all to separate head learning from soul wisdom, the "Eye" from the "Heart" doctrine.

112. Yea, ignorance is like unto a closed and airless vessel; the soul a bird shut up within. It warbles not, nor can it stir a feather; but the songster mute and torpid sits, and of exhaustion dies.

113. But even ignorance is better than head learning with no soul wisdom to illuminate and guide it.

114. The seeds of wisdom cannot sprout and grow in airless space. To live and reap experience the mind needs breadth and depth and points to draw it towards the Diamond Soul.[49] Seek not those points in Maya's realm; but soar beyond illusions, search the eternal and the changeless *Sat*,[50] mistrusting fancy's false suggestions.

115. For mind is like a mirror; it gathers dust while it reflects.[51] It needs the gentle breezes of soul wisdom to brush away the dust of our illusions. Seek, O beginner, to blend thy mind and soul.

116. Shun ignorance, and likewise shun illusion. Avert thy face from world deceptions; mistrust thy senses; they are false. But within thy body—the shrine of thy sensations—seek in the impersonal for the Eternal Man;[52] and having sought him out, look inward: thou art Buddha.[53]

117. Shun praise, O devotee. Praise leads to self-delusion. Thy body is not Self, thy SELF is in itself without a body, and either praise or blame affects it not.

118. Self-gratulation, O disciple, is like unto a lofty tower, up which a haughty fool has climbed. Thereon he sits in prideful solitude and unperceived by any but himself.

119. False learning is rejected by the wise, and scattered to the winds by the good Law. Its wheel revolves for all, the humble and the proud. The Doctrine of the Eye[54] is for the crowd; the Doctrine

of the Heart, for the elect. The first repeat in pride, "Behold, I know"; the last, they who in humbleness have garnered, low confess, "thus have I heard." [55]

120. "Great Sifter" is the name of the Heart Doctrine, O disciple.

121. The wheel of the good Law moves swiftly on. It grinds by night and day. The worthless husks it drives from out the golden grain, the refuse from the flour. The hand of karma guides the wheel; the revolutions mark the beatings of the karmic heart.

122. True knowledge is the flour, false learning is the husk. If thou wouldst eat the bread of wisdom, thy flour thou hast to knead with Amrita's [immortality] clear waters. But if thou kneadest husks with Maya's dew, thou canst create but food for the black doves of death, the birds of birth, decay and sorrow.

123. If thou art told that to become Arhan thou hast to cease to love all beings—tell them they lie.

124. If thou art told that to gain liberation thou hast to hate thy mother and disregard thy son; to disavow thy father and call him "householder";[56] for man and beast all pity to renounce—tell them their tongue is false.

125. Thus teach the Tirthikas, the unbelievers [Brahman ascetics].

126. If thou art taught that sin is born of action and bliss of absolute inaction, then tell them that they err. Nonpermanence of human action; deliverance

of mind from thralldom by the cessation of sin and faults, are not for Deva Egos [the reincarnating Ego]. Thus saith the Doctrine of the Heart.

127. The Dharma of the "Eye" is the embodiment of the external, and the nonexisting.

128. The Dharma of the "Heart" is the embodiment of Bodhi [true, divine wisdom], the permanent and everlasting.

129. The lamp burns bright when wick and oil are clean. To make them clean a cleaner is required. The flame feels not the process of the cleaning. "The branches of a tree are shaken by the wind; the trunk remains unmoved."

130. Both action and inaction may find room in thee; thy body agitated, thy mind tranquil, thy soul as limpid as a mountain lake.

131. Wouldst thou become a Yogi of Time's Circle? Then, O lanoo:

132. Believe thou not that sitting in dark forests, in proud seclusion and apart from men; believe thou not that life on roots and plants, that thirst assuaged with snow from the great Range—believe thou not, O devotee, that this will lead thee to the goal of final liberation.

133. Think not that breaking bone, that rending flesh and muscle, unites thee to thy silent Self.[57] Think not, that when the sins of thy gross form are conquered, O victim of thy shadows,[58] thy duty is accomplished by nature and by man.

**134.** The blessed ones have scorned to do so. The Lion of the Law, the Lord of Mercy [Buddha], perceiving the true cause of human woe, immediately forsook the sweet but selfish rest of quiet wilds. From Aranyaka[59] he became the Teacher of mankind. After Julai[60] had entered the Nirvana, he preached on mount and plain, and held discourses in the cities, to devas, men and gods.[61]

**135.** Sow kindly acts and thou shalt reap their fruition. Inaction in a deed of mercy becomes an action in a deadly sin. Thus saith the Sage.

**136.** Shalt thou abstain from action? Not so shall gain thy soul her freedom. To reach Nirvana one must reach self-knowledge, and self-knowledge is of loving deeds the child.

**137.** Have patience, candidate, as one who fears no failure, courts no success. Fix thy soul's gaze upon the star whose ray thou art,[62] the flaming star that shines within the lightless depths of ever-being, the boundless fields of the unknown.

**138.** Have perseverance as one who doth forevermore endure. Thy shadows live and vanish;[63] that which in thee shall live forever, that which in thee *knows*, for it is knowledge,[64] is not of fleeing life: it is the man that was, that is, and will be, for whom the hour shall never strike.

**139.** If thou wouldst reap sweet peace and rest, disciple, sow with the seeds of merit the fields of future harvests. Accept the woes of birth.

**140**. Step out from sunlight into shade, to make more room for others. The tears that water the parched soil of pain and sorrow, bring forth the blossoms and the fruits of karmic retribution. Out of the furnace of man's life and its black smoke, winged flames arise, flames purified, that soaring onward, beneath the karmic eye, weave in the end the fabric glorified of the three vestures of the Path.[65]

**141**. These vestures are: Nirmanakaya, Sambhogakaya, and Dharmakaya, robe sublime.[66]

**142**. The Shangna robe,[67] 'tis true, can purchase light eternal. The Shangna robe alone gives the Nirvana of destruction; it stops rebirth but, O lanoo, it also kills compassion. No longer can the perfect Buddhas, who don the Dharmakaya glory, help man's salvation. Alas! shall selves be sacrificed to self; mankind, unto the weal of units?

**143**. Know, O beginner, this is the *Open* Path, the way to selfish bliss, shunned by the Bodhisattvas of the Secret Heart, the Buddhas of Compassion.

**144**. To live to benefit mankind is the first step. To practice the six glorious virtues[68] is the second.

**145**. To don Nirmanakaya's humble robe is to forego eternal bliss for self, to help on man's salvation. To reach Nirvana's bliss, but to renounce it, is the supreme, the final step—the highest on renunciation's path.

*146*. Know, O disciple, this is the *Secret* Path, selected by the Buddhas of Perfection, who sacrificed the SELF to weaker Selves.

*147*. Yet, if the Doctrine of the Heart is too high-winged for thee, if thou needest help thyself and fearest to offer help to others—then, thou of timid heart, be warned in time; remain content with the Eye Doctrine of the Law. Hope still. For if the Secret Path is unattainable this day, it is within thy reach tomorrow.[69] Learn that no efforts, not the smallest—whether in right or wrong direction—can vanish from the world of causes. Even wasted smoke remains not traceless. "A harsh word uttered in past lives is not destroyed but ever comes again" [Precepts of the Prasanga School]. The pepper plant will not give birth to roses, nor the sweet jessamine's silver star to thorn or thistle turn.

*148*. Thou canst create this day thy chances for thy morrow. In the Great Journey,[70] causes sown each hour bear each its harvest of effects, for rigid justice rules the world. With mighty sweep of never erring action, it brings to mortals lives of weal or woe, the karmic progeny of all our former thoughts and deeds.

*149*. Take then as much as merit hath in store for thee, O thou of patient heart. Be of good cheer and rest content with fate. Such is thy karma, the karma of the cycle of thy births, the destiny of those, who, in their pain and sorrow, are born along with thee, rejoice and weep from life to life, chained to thy previous actions.

150. Act thou for them today, and they will act for thee tomorrow.

151. 'Tis from the bud of renunciation of the self, that springeth the sweet fruit of final liberation.

152. To perish doomed is he, who out of fear of Mara refrains from helping man, lest he should act for self. The pilgrim who would cool his weary limbs in running waters, yet dares not plunge for terror of the stream, risks to succumb from heat. Inaction based on selfish fear can bear but evil fruit.

153. The selfish devotee lives to no purpose. The man who does not go through his appointed work in life has lived in vain.

154. Follow the wheel of life; follow the wheel of duty to race and kin, to friend and foe, and close thy mind to pleasures as to pain. Exhaust the law of karmic retribution. Gain *siddhis* for thy future birth.

155. If sun thou canst not be, then be the humble planet. Aye, if thou art debarred from flaming like the noonday sun upon the snowcapped mount of purity eternal, then choose, O neophyte, a humbler course.

156. Point out the Way—however dimly, and lost among the host—as does the evening star to those who tread their path in darkness.

157. Behold Migmar [Mars], as in his crimson veils his eye sweeps over slumbering Earth. Behold the fiery aura of the hand of Lhagpa [Mercury] extended in protecting love over the heads of his ascetics. Both are now servants to Nyima [the Sun][71] left in his absence silent watchers in the night. Yet both in Kalpas past were bright Nyimas, and may in future days again become two suns. Such are the falls and rises of the karmic law in nature.

158. Be, O lanoo, like them. Give light and comfort to the toiling pilgrim, and seek out him who knows still less than thou; who in his wretched desolation sits starving for the bread of wisdom and the bread which feeds the shadow, without a Teacher, hope or consolation, and let him hear the Law.

159. Tell him, O candidate, that he who makes of pride and self-regard bondmaidens to devotion; that he who, cleaving to existence, still lays his patience and submission to the Law, as a sweet flower at the feet of *Shakya-Thub-pa* [Buddha], becomes a *Srotapatti*[72] in this birth. The *siddhis* of perfection may loom far, far away; but the first step is taken, the stream is entered, and he may gain the eyesight of the mountain eagle, the hearing of the timid doe.

160. Tell him, O aspirant, that true devotion may bring him back the knowledge, that knowledge

which was his in former births. The deva sight and deva hearing are not obtained in one short birth.

161. Be humble, if thou wouldst attain to wisdom.

162. Be humbler still, when wisdom thou hast mastered.

163. Be like the ocean which receives all streams and rivers. The ocean's mighty calm remains unmoved; it feels them not.

164. Restrain by thy Divine thy lower self.

165. Restrain by the Eternal the Divine.

166. Aye, great is he, who is the slayer of desire.

167. Still greater he, in whom the Self Divine has slain the very knowledge of desire.

168. Guard thou the lower lest it soil the Higher.

169. The way to final freedom is within thy Self.

170. That way begins and ends outside of self.[73]

171. Unpraised by men and humble is the mother of all rivers, in Tirthika's proud sight; empty the human form though filled with Amrita's sweet waters, in the sight of fools. Withal, the birthplace of the sacred rivers is the sacred land,[74] and he who wisdom hath, is honored by all men.

172. Arhans and Sages of the boundless vision[75] are rare as is the blossom of the Udumbara tree. Arhans are born at midnight hour, together with the sacred plant of nine and seven stalks,[76] the holy flower that opens and blooms in darkness, out of the pure dew and on the frozen bed of snowcapped heights, heights that are trodden by no sinful foot.

173. No Arhan, O lanoo, becomes one in that birth when for the first the soul begins to long for final liberation. Yet, O thou anxious one, no warrior volunteering fight in the fierce strife between the living and the dead,[77] not one recruit, can ever be refused the right to enter on the Path that leads toward the field of battle.

174. For either he shall win, or he shall fall.

175. Yea, if he conquers, Nirvana shall be his. Before he casts his shadow off his mortal coil—that pregnant cause of anguish and illimitable pain—in him will men a great and holy Buddha honor.

176. And if he falls, even then he does not fall in vain; the enemies he slew in the last battle will not return to life in the next birth that will be his.

177. But if thou wouldst Nirvana reach, or cast the prize away,[78] let not the fruit of action and inaction be thy motive, thou of dauntless heart.

178. Know that the Bodhisattva who liberation changes for renunciation to don the miseries of "Secret Life"[79] is called "thrice honored," O thou candidate for woe throughout the cycles.

*179*. The Path is one, disciple, yet in the end, twofold. Marked are its stages by four and seven portals. At one end—bliss immediate, and at the other—bliss deferred. Both are of merit the reward: the choice is thine.

*180*. The one becomes the two, the Open and the Secret.[80] The first one leadeth to the goal, the second, to self-immolation.

*181*. When to the Permanent is sacrificed the mutable, the prize is thine: the drop returneth whence it came. The Open Path leads to the changeless change—Nirvana, the glorious state of Absoluteness, the Bliss past human thought.

*182*. Thus, the first Path is liberation.

*183*. But Path the second is renunciation and therefore called the "Path of Woe."

*184*. That Secret Path leads the Arhan to mental woe unspeakable; woe for the living dead,[81] and helpless pity for the men of karmic sorrow, the fruit of karma sages dare not still.

*185*. For it is written: "Teach to eschew all causes; the ripple of effect, as the great tidal wave, thou shalt let run its course."

*186*. The Open Way, no sooner has thou reached its goal, will lead thee to reject the Bodhisattvic body and make thee enter the thrice glorious state of Dharmakaya,[82] which is oblivion of the world and men forever.

**187.** The Secret Way leads also to Paranirvanic bliss—but at the close of Kalpas without number; Nirvanas gained and lost from boundless pity and compassion for the world of deluded mortals.

**188.** But it is said, "The last shall be the greatest"; *Samyak Sambuddha,* the Teacher of Perfection, gave up his Self for the salvation of the world, by stopping at the threshold of Nirvana—the pure state.

**189.** Thou hast the knowledge now concerning the two Ways. Thy time will come for choice, O thou of eager soul, when thou hast reached the end and passed the seven Portals. Thy mind is clear. No more art thou entangled in delusive thoughts, for thou hast learned all. Unveiled stands truth and looks thee sternly in the face. She says:

**190.** "Sweet are the fruits of rest and liberation for the sake of Self; but sweeter still the fruits of long and bitter duty. Aye, renunciation for the sake of others, of suffering fellow men."

**191.** He who becomes Pratyeka Buddha[83] makes his obeisance but to his Self. The Bodhisattva who has won the battle, who holds the prize within his palm, yet says in his divine compassion:

**192.** "For others' sake this great reward I yield" —accomplishes the greater renunciation.

**193**.  A Savior of the World is he.

**194**.  Behold! The goal of bliss and the long Path of Woe are at the furthest end. Thou canst choose either, O aspirant to Sorrow, throughout the coming cycles! . . .

**195**.  OM VAJRAPANI HUM.

# FRAGMENT THREE
## The Seven Portals

**196.** Upadhyaya,[84] the choice is made, I thirst for wisdom. Now hast thou rent the veil before the secret Path and taught the greater Yana.[85] Thy servant here is ready for thy guidance.

**197.** 'Tis well, Shravaka.[86] Prepare thyself, for thou wilt have to travel on alone. The Teacher can but point the way. The Path is one for all, the means to reach the goal must vary with the pilgrims.

**198.** Which wilt thou choose, O thou of dauntless heart? The Samtan[87] of Eye Doctrine, fourfold Dhyana, or thread thy way through Paramitas,[88] six in number, noble gates of virtue leading to Bodhi and to Prajna, seventh step of wisdom?

**199.** The rugged Path of fourfold Dhyana winds on uphill. Thrice great is he who climbs the lofty top.

**200.** The Paramita heights are crossed by a still steeper path. Thou hast to fight thy way through portals seven, seven strongholds held by cruel, crafty powers—passions incarnate.

**201**. Be of good cheer, disciple; bear in mind the golden rule. Once thou has passed the gate Srotapatti,[89] "he who the stream hath entered," once thy foot hath pressed the bed of the Nirvanic stream in this or any future life, thou hast but seven other births before thee, O thou of adamantine will.

**202**. Look on. What see'st thou before thine eye, O aspirant to godlike wisdom?

**203**. "The cloak of darkness is upon the deep of matter; within its folds I struggle. Beneath my gaze it deepens, Lord; it is dispelled beneath the waving of thy hand. A shadow moveth, creeping like the stretching serpent coils. . . . It grows, swells out, and disappears in darkness."

**204**. It is the shadow of thyself outside the Path, cast on the darkness of thy sins.

**205**. "Yea, Lord; I see the Path; its foot in mire, its summits lost in glorious light Nirvanic. And now I see the ever narrowing Portals on the hard and thorny way to Jnana [Knowledge, Wisdom]."

**206**. Thou seest well, lanoo. These Portals lead the aspirant across the waters on to the other shore.[90] Each Portal hath a golden key that openeth its gate; and these keys are:

**207**. (1) DANA, the key of charity and love immortal.

*208*. (2) SHILA, the key of harmony in word and act, the key that counterbalances the cause and the effect, and leaves no further room for karmic action.

*209*. (3) KSHANTI, patience sweet, that naught can ruffle.

*210*. (4) VIRAGA, indifference to pleasure and to pain, illusion conquered, truth alone perceived.

*211*. (5) VIRYA, the dauntless energy that fights its way to the supernal truth, out of the mire of lies terrestrial.

*212*. (6) DHYANA, whose golden gate once opened leads the Naljor [a saint, an adept] toward the realm of *Sat* eternal and its ceaseless contemplation.

*213*. (7) PRAJNA, the key to which makes of a man a god, creating him a Bodhisattva, son of the Dhyanis.

*214*. Such to the Portals are the golden keys.

*215*. Before thou canst approach the last, O weaver of thy freedom, thou hast to master these Paramitas of perfection—the virtues transcendental six and ten in number—along the weary Path.

*216*. For, O disciple! Before thou wert made fit to meet thy Teacher face to face, thy Master light to light, what wert thou told?

*217*. Before thou canst approach the foremost gate, thou hast to learn to part thy body from thy mind, to dissipate the shadow, and to live in the eternal. For this, thou hast to live and breathe in all, as all that thou perceivest breathes in thee; to feel thyself abiding in all things, all things in Self.

*218.* Thou shalt not let thy senses make a playground of thy mind.

*219.* Thou shalt not separate thy being from BEING, and the rest, but merge the Ocean in the drop, the drop within the Ocean.

*220.* So shalt thou be in full accord with all that lives; bear love to men as though they were thy brother pupils, disciples of one Teacher, the sons of one sweet mother.

*221.* Of teachers there are many; the MASTER-SOUL is one,[91] *Alaya,* the Universal Soul. Live in that MASTER as Its ray in thee. Live in thy fellows as they live in It.

*222.* Before thou standest on the threshold of the Path, before thou crossest the foremost gate, thou hast to merge the two into the One and sacrifice the personal to SELF impersonal, and thus destroy the path between the two—*antahkarana.*[92]

*223.* Thou hast to be prepared to answer Dharma, the stern law, whose voice will ask thee at thy first, at thy initial, step:

*224.* "Hast thou complied with all the rules, O thou of lofty hopes?"

225. "Hast thou attuned thy heart and mind to the great mind and heart of all mankind? For as the sacred river's roaring voice whereby all nature sounds are echoed back,[93] so must the heart of him 'who in the stream would enter,' thrill in response to every sigh and thought of all that lives and breathes."

226. Disciples may be likened to the strings of the soul-echoing vina; mankind, unto its sounding board; the hand that sweeps it to the tuneful breath of the Great World-Soul. The string that fails to answer beneath the Master's touch in dulcet harmony with all the others, breaks—and is cast away. So the collective minds of lanoo-shravakas. They have to be attuned to the Upadhyaya's mind—one with the Over-Soul—or, break away.

227. Thus do the "Brothers of the Shadow"—the murderers of their Souls, the dread Dad-Dugpa clan.[94]

228. Hast thou attuned thy being to humanity's great pain, O candidate for light?

229. Thou hast? . . . Thou mayest enter. Yet, ere thou settest foot upon the dreary Path of sorrow, 'tis well thou shouldst first learn the pitfalls on thy way.

230. Armed with the key of charity, of love and tender mercy, thou art secure before the gate of Dana, the gate that standeth at the entrance of the Path.

231. Behold, O happy pilgrim! The portal that faceth thee is high and wide, seems easy of access. The road that leads therethrough is straight and smooth and green. 'Tis like a sunny glade in the dark forest depths, a spot on earth mirrored from Amitabha's paradise. There, nightingales of hope and birds of radiant plumage sing perched in green bowers, chanting success to fearless pilgrims. They sing of Bodhisattvas' virtues five, the fivefold source of Bodhi power, and of the seven steps in knowledge.

232. Pass on! For thou has brought the key; thou art secure.

233. And to the second gate the way is verdant too. But it is steep and winds uphill; yea, to its rocky top. Gray mists will overhang its rough and stony height, and all be dark beyond. As on he goes, the song of hope soundeth more feeble in the pilgrim's heart. The thrill of doubt is now upon him; his step less steady grows.

234. Beware of this, O candidate! Beware of fear that spreadeth, like the black and soundless wings of midnight bat, between the moonlight of thy soul and thy great goal that loometh in the distance far away.

235. Fear, O disciple, kills the will and stays all action. If lacking in the Shila virtue, the pilgrim trips, and karmic pebbles bruise his feet along the rocky path.

236. Be of sure foot, O candidate. In Kshanti's [patience] essence bathe thy Soul; for now thou dost

approach the portal of that name, the gate of fortitude and patience.

*237*. Close not thine eyes, nor lose thy sight of Dorje;[95] Mara's arrows ever smite the man who has not reached Viraga.[96]

*238*. Beware of trembling. Beneath the breath of fear the key of Kshanti rusty grows: the rusty key refuseth to unlock.

*239*. The more thou dost advance, the more thy feet pitfalls will meet. The path that leadeth on, is lighted by one fire—the light of daring, burning in the heart. The more one dares, the more he shall obtain. The more he fears, the more that light shall pale—and that alone can guide. For as the lingering sunbeam, that on the top of some tall mountain shines, is followed by black night when out it fades, so is heart-light. When out it goes, a dark and threatening shade will fall from thine own heart upon the path, and root thy feet in terror to the spot.

*240*. Beware, disciple, of that lethal shade. No light that shines from Spirit can dispel the darkness of the nether soul, unless all selfish thought has fled therefrom, and that the pilgrim saith: "I have renounced this passing frame; I have destroyed the cause: the shadows cast can, as effects, no longer be." For now the last great fight, the final war between the Higher and the Lower Self, hath taken place. Behold, the very battlefield is now engulfed in the great war, and is no more.

241. But once that thou hast passed the gate of Kshanti, step the third is taken. Thy body is thy slave. Now, for the fourth prepare, the portal of temptations which do ensnare the inner man.

242. Ere thou canst near that goal, before thine hand is lifted to upraise the fourth gate's latch, thou must have mustered all the mental changes in thy self and slain the army of the thought sensations that, subtle and insidious, creep unasked within the Soul's bright shrine.

243. If thou wouldst not be slain by them, then must thou harmless make thy own creations, the children of thy thoughts, unseen, impalpable, that swarm round humankind, the progeny and heirs to man and his terrestrial spoils. Thou hast to study the voidness of the seeming full, the fullness of the seeming void. O fearless aspirant, look deep within the well of thine own heart, and answer. Knowest thou of Self the powers, O thou perceiver of external shadows?

244. If thou dost not—then art thou lost.

245. For, on Path fourth, the lightest breeze of passion or desire will stir the steady light upon the pure white walls of Soul. The smallest wave of longing or regret for Maya's gifts illusive, along *Antahkarana*—the path that lies between thy Spirit and thy self, the highway of sensations, the rude arousers of *Ahamkara*[97]—a thought as fleeting as the lightning flash will make thee thy three prizes forfeit—the prizes thou has won.

246. For know, that the Eternal knows no change.

247. "The eight dire miseries forsake forevermore. If not, to wisdom, sure, thou canst not come, nor yet to liberation," saith the great Lord, the Tathagata of perfection, he who has followed in the footsteps of his predecessors.[98]

248. Stern and exacting is the virtue of Viraga. If thou its path wouldst master, thou must keep thy mind and thy perceptions far freer than before from killing action.

249. Thou hast to saturate thyself with pure Alaya, become as one with Nature's Soul-Thought. At one with it thou art invincible; in separation, thou becomest the playground of Samvriti,[99] origin of all the world's delusions.

250. All is impermanent in man except the pure bright essence of Alaya. Man is its crystal ray: a beam of light immaculate within, a form of clay material upon the lower surface. That beam is thy life-guide and thy true Self, the Watcher and silent Thinker, the victim of thy lower self. Thy Soul cannot be hurt but through thy erring body; control and master both, and thou art safe when crossing to the nearing Gate of Balance.

251. Be of good cheer, O daring pilgrim to the other shore. Heed not the whisperings of Mara's hosts; wave off the tempters, those ill-natured sprites, the jealous Lhamayin[100] in endless space.

**252.** Hold firm! Thou nearest now the middle portal, the gate of woe, with its ten thousand snares.

**253.** Have mastery o'er thy thoughts, O striver for perfection, if thou wouldst cross its threshold.

**254.** Have mastery o'er thy soul, O seeker after truths undying, if thou wouldst reach the goal.

**255.** Thy soul-gaze center on the One Pure Light, the Light that is free from affection, and use thy golden key.

**256.** The dreary task is done, thy labor well-nigh o'er. The wide abyss that gaped to swallow thee is almost spanned.

**257.** Thou has now crossed the moat that circles round the gate of human passions. Thou hast now conquered Mara and his furious host.

**258.** Thou hast removed pollution from thine heart and bled it from impure desire. But, O thou glorious combatant, thy task is not yet done. Build high, lanoo, the wall that shall hedge in the Holy Isle [the Higher Ego, or Thinking Self], the dam that will protect thy mind from pride and satisfaction at thoughts of the great feat achieved.

259. A sense of pride would mar the work. Aye, build it strong, lest the fierce rush of battling waves that mount and beat its shore from out the great world Maya's ocean, swallow up the pilgrim and the isle— yea, even when the victory's achieved.

260. Thine "isle" is the deer, thy thoughts the hounds that weary and pursue his progress to the stream of Life. Woe to the deer that is o'ertaken by the barking fiends before he reach the Vale of Refuge— *Jnana Marga*, "path of pure knowledge" named.

261. Ere thou canst settle in Jnana Marga[101] and call it thine, thy Soul has to become as the ripe mango fruit: as soft and sweet as its bright golden pulp for others' woes, as hard as that fruit's stone for thine own throes and sorrows, O conqueror of weal and woe.

262. Make hard thy Soul against the snares of self; deserve for it the name of "Diamond Soul."[102]

263. For, as the diamond buried deep within the throbbing heart of earth can never mirror back the earthly lights; so are thy mind and Soul; plunged in Jnana Marga, these must mirror naught of Maya's realm illusive.

264. When thou hast reached that state, the Portals that thou hast to conquer on the path fling open wide their gates to let thee pass, and Nature's

strongest mights possess no power to stay thy course. Thou wilt be master of the sevenfold Path: but not till then, O candidate for trials passing speech.

265. Till then, a task far harder still awaits thee: thou hast to feel thyself ALL-THOUGHT, and yet exile all thoughts from out thy Soul.

266. Thou hast to reach that fixity of mind in which no breeze, however strong, can waft an earthly thought within. Thus purified, the shrine must of all action, sound, or earthly light be void; even as the butterfly, overtaken by the frost, falls lifeless at the threshold—so must all earthly thoughts fall dead before the fane.

Behold it written:

267. "Ere the gold flame can burn with steady light, the lamp must stand well-guarded in a spot free from all wind" [Bhagavad Gita]. Exposed to shifting breeze, the jet will flicker and the quivering flame cast shades deceptive, dark and ever-changing, on the Soul's white shrine.

268. And then, O thou pursuer of the truth, thy mind-soul will become as a mad elephant that rages in the jungle. Mistaking forest trees for living foes, he perishes in his attempts to kill the ever-shifting shadows dancing on the wall of sunlit rocks.

269. Beware, lest in the care of self thy Soul should lose her foothold on the soil of Deva knowledge.

*270.* Beware, lest in forgetting Self, thy soul lose o'er its trembling mind control, and forfeit thus the due fruition of its conquests.

*271.* Beware of change! For change is thy great foe. This change will fight thee off, and throw thee back, out of the Path thou treadest, deep into viscous swamps of doubt.

*272.* Prepare and be forewarned in time. If thou hast tried and failed, O dauntless fighter, yet lose not courage: fight on and to the charge return again, and yet again.

*273.* The fearless warrior, his precious life blood oozing from his wide and gaping wounds, will still attack the foe, drive him from out his stronghold, vanquish him, ere he himself expires. Act then, all ye who fail and suffer, act like him; and from the stronghold of your soul, chase all your foes away—ambition, anger, hatred, even to the shadow of desire—when even you have failed. . . .

*274.* Remember, thou that fightest for man's liberation,[103] each failure is success, and each sincere attempt wins its reward in time. The holy germs that sprout and grow unseen in the disciple's soul, their stalks wax strong at each new trial, they bend like reeds but never break, nor can they ever be lost. But when the hour has struck they blossom forth.[104]

*275*. But if thou camest prepared, then have no fear.

*276*. Henceforth thy way is clear right through the Virya gate, the fifth one of the Seven Portals. Thou art now on the way that leadeth to the Dhyana haven, the sixth, the Bodhi Portal.

*277*. The Dhyana gate is like an alabaster vase, white and transparent; within there burns a steady golden fire, the flame of prajna that radiates from Atman.

*278*. Thou art that vase.

*279*. Thou has estranged thyself from objects of the senses, traveled on the "Path of seeing," on the "Path of hearing," and standest in the light of Knowledge. Thou hast now reached Titiksha state.[105]

*280*. O Naljor, thou art safe.

*281*. Know, conqueror of sins, once that a Sowani[106] hath crossed the seventh Path, all Nature thrills with joyous awe and feels subdued. The silver star now twinkles out the news to the night blossoms, the streamlet to the pebbles ripples out the tale; dark ocean waves will roar it to the rocks surf-bound, scent-laden breezes sing it to the vales, and stately pines mysteriously whisper: "A Master has arisen, a Master of the Day."[107]

282. He standeth now like a white pillar to the west, upon whose face the rising sun of thought eternal poureth forth its first most glorious waves. His mind, like a becalmed and boundless ocean, spreadeth out in shoreless space. He holdeth life and death in his strong hand.

283. Yea, he is mighty. The living power made free in him, that power which is himself, can raise the tabernacle of illusion high above the gods, above great Brahma and Indra. *Now* he shall surely reach his great reward!

284. Shall he not use the gifts which it confers for his own rest and bliss, his well-earned weal and glory—he, the subduer of the great delusion?

285. Nay, O thou candidate for Nature's hidden lore! If one would follow in the steps of holy Tathagata, those gifts and powers are not for self.

286. Wouldst thou thus dam the waters born on Sumeru?[108] Shalt thou divert the stream for thine own sake, or send it back to its prime source along the crests of cycles?

287. If thou wouldst have that stream of hard-earned knowledge, of Wisdom heaven-born, remain sweet running waters, thou shouldst not leave it to become a stagnant pond.

**288**. Know, if of Amitabha, the "Boundless Age," thou wouldst become coworker, then must thou shed the light acquired, like to the Bodhisattvas twain,[109] upon the span of all three worlds.[110]

**289**. Know that the stream of superhuman knowledge and the Deva wisdom thou hast won, must, from thyself, the channel of Alaya, be poured forth into another bed.

**290**. Know, O Naljor, thou of the Secret Path, its pure fresh waters must be used to sweeter make the ocean's bitter waves—that mighty sea of sorrow formed of the tears of men.

**291**. Alas! when once thou has become like the fixed star in highest heaven, that bright celestial orb must shine from out the spatial depths for all— save for itself; give light to all, but take from none.

**292**. Alas! when once thou hast become like the pure snow in mountain vales, cold and unfeeling to the touch, warm and protective to the seed that sleepeth deep beneath its bosom—'tis now that snow which must receive the biting frost, the northern blasts, thus shielding from their sharp and cruel tooth the earth that holds the promised harvest, the harvest that will feed the hungry.

**293**. Self-doomed to live through future kalpas [cycles of ages], unthanked and unperceived by men; wedged as a stone with countless other stones which form the "Guardian Wall,"[111] such is thy future if the seventh gate thou passest. Built by the hands of many

Masters of Compassion, raised by their tortures, by their blood cemented, it shields mankind, since man is man, protecting it from further and far greater misery and sorrow.

294. Withal, man sees it not, will not perceive it, nor will he heed the word of Wisdom . . . for he knows it not.

295. But thou hast heard it, thou knowest all, O thou of eager guileless Soul . . . and thou must choose. Then hearken yet again.

296. On Sowan's Path, O Srotapatti, thou art secure. Aye, on that Marga [Path], where naught but darkness meets the weary pilgrim, where torn by thorns the hands drip blood, the feet are cut by sharp unyielding flints, and Mara wields his strongest arms—there lies a great reward *immediately* beyond.

297. Calm and unmoved the pilgrim glideth up the stream that to Nirvana leads. He knoweth that the more his feet will bleed, the whiter will himself be washed. He knoweth well that after seven short and fleeting births Nirvana will be his. . . .

298. Such is the Dhyana Path, the haven of the Yogi, the blessed goal that Srotapattis crave.

299. Not so when he hath crossed and won the Arhat path.

300. There Klesha[112] is destroyed forever, Tanha's[113] roots torn out. But stay, disciple . . . Yet, one word. Canst thou destroy divine compassion?

Compassion is no attribute. It is the Law of laws —eternal harmony, Alaya's Self, a shoreless universal essence, the light of everlasting right, and fitness of all things, the law of love eternal.

301. The more thou dost become at one with it, thy being melted in its Being, the more thy soul unites with that which IS, the more thou wilt become compassion absolute.[114]

302. Such is the Arya Path, Path of the Buddhas of perfection.

303. Withal, what mean the sacred scrolls which make thee say:

304. "OM! I believe it is not all the Arhats that get of the Nirvanic Path the sweet fruition."

305. "OM! I believe that the Nirvana-Dharma is entered not by all the Buddhas."[115]

306. "Yea; on the Arya Path thou art no more Srotapatti, thou art a Bodhisattva.[116] The stream is crossed. 'Tis true thou hast a right to Dharmakaya vesture, but Sambhogakaya is greater than a Nirvani, and greater still is a Nirmanakaya—the Buddha of Compassion."[117]

307. Now bend thy head and listen well, O Bodhisattva—Compassion speaks and saith: "Can there be bliss when all that lives must suffer? Shalt thou be saved and hear the whole world cry?"

308. Now thou hast heard that which was said.

*309*. Thou shalt attain the seventh step and cross the gate of final knowledge but only to wed woe—if thou wouldst be Tathagata, follow upon thy predecessor's steps, remain unselfish till the endless end.

*310*. Thou art enlightened—choose thy way.

*311*. Behold, the mellow light that floods the eastern sky. In signs of praise both heaven and earth unite. And from the fourfold manifested powers a chant of love ariseth, both from the flaming fire and flowing water, and from sweet-smelling earth and rushing wind.

*312*. Hark! . . . from the deep unfathomable vortex of that golden light in which the victor bathes, All Nature's wordless voice in thousand tones ariseth to proclaim:

*313*. JOY UNTO YE, O MEN OF MYALBA.[118]

*314*. A PILGRIM HATH RETURNED BACK FROM THE OTHER SHORE.

*315*. A NEW ARHAN[119] IS BORN. . . .

*316*. *Peace to all beings.*[120]

# NOTES

1. The Pali word *iddhi* is the synonym of the Sanskrit *siddhis*, or psychic faculties, the abnormal powers in man. There are two kinds of siddhis. One group which embraces the lower, coarse, psychic, and mental energies; the other is one which exacts the highest training of spiritual powers. Says Krishna in *Shrimad Bhagavata:* "He who is engaged in the performance of yoga, who has subdued his senses and who has concentrated his mind in me (Krishna), such yogis all the siddhis stand ready to serve."

2. The "Soundless Voice," or the "Voice of the Silence." Literally perhaps this would read "Voice in the Spiritual Sound," as *nada* is the equivalent word in Sanskrit for the Senzar term.

3. *Dharana* is the intense and perfect concentration of the mind upon some one interior object, accompanied by complete abstraction from everything pertaining to the external universe, or the world of the senses.

4. The "great Master" is the term used by *lanoos* or chelas to indicate one's Higher Self. It is the equivalent of *Avalokiteshvara*, and the same as *Adi-Budha* with the Buddhist occultists; *Atman*, the "Self" (the Higher Self) with the Brahmanas; and *Christos* with the ancient Gnostics.

5. Soul is used here for the human ego or manas, that which is referred to in our occult septenary division as the human soul in contradistinction to the spiritual and animal souls.

6. *Maha Maya*, "Great Illusion," the objective universe.

7. *Sakkayaditthi*, "delusion" of personality.

8. *Attavada*, the heresy of the belief in soul or rather in the separateness of soul or self from the one universal, infinite Self.

9. The *Tattvajnani* is the "knower" or discriminator of the principles in nature and in man; and *Atmajnani* is the knower of Atman or the universal, One Self.

10. *Kala Hamsa*, the Bird or Swan. Says the Nada-Bindu Upanishad (Rig Veda): "The syllable A is considered to be its (the bird Hamsa's) right wing, U, its left, M, its tail, and the ardha-matra (half meter) is said to be its head."

11. Eternity with the Orientals has quite another signification than it has with us. It stands generally for the 100 years or "age" of Brahma, the duration of a kalpa or a period of 4,320,000,000 years. [According to *The Secret Doctrine*, the figures given in this note are those of a "day" of Brahma; an "age" of Brahma is a Maha-kalpa of 311,040,000,000,000 years.]

12. Says the same Nada-Bindu, "A Yogi who bestrides the Hamsa (thus contemplates on Aum) is not affected by karmic influences or crores of sins."

13. Give up the life of physical personality if you would live in spirit.

14. The three states of consciousness, which are *jagrat*, the waking; *svapna*, the dreaming; and *sushupti*, the deep sleeping state. These three yogic conditions, lead to the fourth, or—

15. The *turiya,* that beyond the dreamless state, the one above all, a state of high spiritual consciousness.

16. Some Sanskrit mystics locate seven planes of being, the seven spiritual *lokas* or worlds within the body of *Kala Hamsa,* the Swan out of time and space, convertible into the Swan *in* time, when it becomes Brahma, instead of Brahman.

17. The phenomenal world of senses and of terrestrial consciousness only.

18. The astral region, the psychic world of supersensuous perceptions and of deceptive sights—the world of mediums. It is the great "astral serpent" of Éliphas Lévi. No blossom plucked in those regions has ever yet been brought down on earth without its serpent coiled around the stem. It is the world of the Great Illusion.

19. The region of the full spiritual consciousness beyond which there is no longer danger for him who has reached it.

20. The initiate who leads the disciple through the knowledge given to him to his spiritual or second birth is called the father guru or Master.

21. *Ajnana* is ignorance or non-wisdom, the opposite of knowledge, jnana.

22. *Mara* is in exoteric religions a demon, an *asura,* but in esoteric philosophy it is personified temptation through men's vices, and translated literally means "that which kills" the soul. It is represented as a king (of the Maras) with a crown in which shines a jewel of such luster that it blinds those who look at it, this luster referring of course to the fascination exercised by vice upon certain natures.

23. The *inner* chamber of the Heart, called in Sanskrit *Brahma-pura.* The "fiery power" is kundalini.

24. The "power" and the "World Mother" are names given to *kundalini*—one of the mystic yogic powers. It is buddhi considered as an active instead of a passive principle (which it is generally, when regarded only as the vehicle, or casket of the Supreme Spirit, Atma). It is an electro-spiritual force, a creative power which when aroused into action can as easily kill as it can create.

25. *Khechara* or "sky-walker" or "goer." As explained in the 6th *adhyaya* of that king of mystic works the *Jnaneshvari*—the body of the Yogi becomes as one *formed of the wind*; as "a cloud from which limbs have sprouted out," after which—"he (the Yogi) beholds the things beyond the seas and stars; he hears the language of the Devas and comprehends it, and perceives what is passing in the mind of the ant."

26. *Vina* is an Indian stringed instrument like a lute.

27. The six principles; meaning when the lower personality is destroyed and the inner individuality is merged into and lost in the seventh or Spirit.

28. The disciple is one with Brahman or the Atman.

29. The astral form produced by the kamic principle, the *kama-rupa* or body of desire.

30. *Manasa-rupa.* The first refers to the astral or personal self; the second to the individuality or the reincarnating Ego whose consciousness on our plane or the lower manas has to be paralyzed.

31. *Kundalini* is called the "serpentine" or the annular power on account of its spiral-like working or progress in the body of the ascetic developing the power in himself. It is an electric fiery occult or fohatic power, the great pristine force, which underlies all organic and inorganic matter.

32. This Path is mentioned in all the mystic works. As Krishna says in the *Jnaneshvari:* "When this Path is beheld . . . whether one sets out to the bloom of the east or to the chambers of the west, *without moving,* O holder of the bow, *is the traveling in this road.* In this path, to whatever place one would go, *that place one's own self* becomes." "Thou art the Path" is said to the adept guru and by the latter to the disciple, after initiation. "I am the way and the Path," says another Master.

33. Adeptship—the "blossom of *Bodhisattva.*"

34. *Tanha*—"the will to live," the fear of death and love for life, that force or energy which causes the rebirths.

35. These mystic sounds or the melody heard by the ascetic at the beginning of his cycle of meditation called *anahatashabda* by the yogis.

36. This means that in the sixth stage of development, which in the occult system is *Dharana,* every sense as an individual faculty has to be "killed" (or paralyzed) on this plane, passing into and merging with the *seventh* sense, the most spiritual.

37. See note 3 above.

38. Every stage of development in Raja Yoga is symbolized by a geometrical figure. This one is the sacred triangle, and precedes *Dharana*. The △ is the sign of the high chelas, while another kind of triangle is that of high Initiates. It is the symbol "I" discoursed upon by Buddha and used by him as a symbol of the embodied form of Tathagata when released from the three methods of the *prajna*. Once the preliminary and lower stages passed, the disciple sees no more the △ but the — the abbreviation of the —, the full Septenary. *Its true form is not given here, as it is almost sure to be pounced upon by some charlatans* and desecrated in its use for fraudulent purposes.

39. The star that burns overhead is "the star of initiation." The castemark of Shaivas, or devotees of the sect of Shiva, the great patron of all yogis, is a black round spot, the symbol of the sun now, perhaps, but that of the star of initiation, in Occultism, in days of old.

40. The basis (*upadhi*) of the ever unreachable Flame, so long as the ascetic is still in this life.

41. *Dhyana* is the last stage before the final *on this Earth* unless one becomes a full Mahatma. As said already, in this state the Raja Yogi is yet spiritually conscious of self, and the working of his higher principles. One step more, and he will be on the plane beyond the seventh (or fourth according to some schools). These, after the practice of *pratyahara*—a preliminary training, in order to control one's mind and thoughts—count Dharana, Dhyana, and Samadhi and embraces the three under the generic name of Samyama.

42. *Samadhi* is the state in which the ascetic loses the consciousness of every individuality including his own. He becomes the ALL.

43. The four modes of truth are, in Northern Buddhism, *Ku* "suffering or misery"; *Tu* "the assembling of temptations"; *Mu* "their destructions"; and *Tao*, the "Path." The five impediments are the knowledge of misery, truth about human frailty, oppressive restraints, and the absolute necessity of separation from all the ties of passion and even of desires. The Path of Salvation is the last one.

44. At the portal of the assembling, the King of the Maras (the *Maha Mara*) stands trying to blind the candidate by the radiance of his "jewel."

45. This is the fourth path out of the five paths of rebirth which lead and toss all human beings into perpetual states of sorrow and joy. These paths are but subdivisions of the one, the path followed by karma.

46. The two schools of Buddha's doctrine, the esoteric and the exoteric, are respectively called the "Heart" and the "Eye" Doctrine. Bodhidharma called them in China—from whence the names reached Tibet—the *Tsung-men* (esoteric) and *Kiau-men* (exoteric school). It [the Heart Doctrine] is so named because it is the teaching which emanated from Gautama Buddha's *heart,* whereas the Eye Doctrine was the work of his head or brain. The Heart Doctrine is also called the "seal of truth" or the "true seal," a symbol found on the heading of almost all esoteric works.

47. The "tree of knowledge" is a title given by the followers of the *Bodhidharma* (Wisdom Religion) to those who have attained the height of mystic knowledge—adepts. Nagarjuna, the founder of the Madhyamika school, was called the "Dragon Tree," dragon standing as a symbol of wisdom and knowledge. The tree is honored because it is under the Bodhi (wisdom) tree that Buddha received his birth and enlightenment, preached his first sermon, and died.

48. "Secret Heart" is the esoteric doctrine.

49. "Diamond Soul," Vajrasattva, a title of the supreme Buddha, the Lord of all Mysteries, called Vajradhara and Adi-Buddha.

50. *Sat,* the one eternal and absolute Reality and Truth, all the rest being illusion.

51. From *Shin-Sien's* doctrine, who teaches that the human mind is like a mirror which attracts and reflects every atom of dust, and has to be, like that mirror, watched over and dusted every day. *Shin-Sien* was the sixth Patriarch of North China who taught the esoteric doctrine of Bodhidharma.

52. The reincarnating EGO is called by the Northern Buddhists the "true man," who becomes in union with his Higher Self, a Buddha.

53. "Buddha" means "Enlightened."

54. See note 46. The *exoteric* Buddhism of the masses.

55. The usual formula that precedes the Buddhist scriptures, meaning that that which follows is what has been recorded by direct oral tradition from Buddha and the Arhats.

56. Rathapala the great Arhat thus addresses his father in the legend called *Rathapala Sutrasanne*. But as all such legends are allegorical (*e.g.* Rathapala's father has a mansion with seven doors) hence the reproof, to those who accept them literally.

57. The Higher Self, the seventh principle.

58. Our physical bodies are called "shadows" in the mystic schools.

59. A hermit who retires to the jungles and lives in a forest, when becoming a Yogi.

60. *Julai,* the Chinese name for Tathagata, a title applied to every Buddha.

61. All the Northern and Southern traditions agree in showing Buddha quitting his solitude as soon as he had resolved the problem of life—i.e., received the inner enlightenment—and teaching mankind publicly.

62. Every spiritual EGO is a ray of a Planetary Spirit according to esoteric teaching.

63. "Personalities" or physical bodies called "shadows" are evanescent.

64. Mind (*Manas*), the thinking principle or Ego in man, is referred to as Knowledge itself, because the human Egos are called *Manasa-putras*, the sons of (universal) Mind.

65. See note 117, verse 306.

66. See note 117, verse 306.

67. The Shangna robe, from Shangnavesu of Rajagriha, the third great Arhat or Patriarch as the Orientalists call the hierarchy of the 33 Arhats who spread Buddhism. *Shangna robe* means, metaphorically, the acquirement of wisdom with which the Nirvana of destruction (of personality) is entered. Literally, the initiation robe of the neophytes. Edkins states that this "grass cloth" was brought to China from Tibet in the Tang Dynasty. "When an Arhan is born this plant is found growing in a clean spot," says the Chinese as also the Tibetan legend.

68. To "practice the Paramita Path" means to become a Yogi with a view of becoming an ascetic.

69. Tomorrow means the following rebirth or reincarnation.

70. The "Great Journey" is the whole complete cycle of existences, in one "Round."

71. *Nyima,* the sun in Tibetan astrology. *Migmar* or Mars is symbolized by an eye and *Lhagpa* or Mercury by a hand.

72. Srotapatti or "he who enters in the stream" of Nirvana, unless he reaches the goal owing to some exceptional reasons, can rarely attain Nirvana in one birth. Usually a chela is said to begin the ascending effort in one life and end or reach it only in his seventh succeeding birth.

73. Meaning the personal lower self.

74. *Tirthikas* are the Brahmanical sectarians, beyond the Himalayas called infidels by the Buddhists in the sacred land, Tibet, and vice versa.

75. Boundless vision or psychic, superhuman sight. An Arhan is credited with seeing and knowing all at a distance as well as on the spot.

76. See note 67 above, Shangna plant.

77. The "living" is the immortal higher Ego, and the "dead"—the lower personal ego.

78. See note 117, verse 306.

79. The "Secret Life" is life as a Nirmanakaya.

80. The "Open" and the "Secret Path"—or the one taught to the layman, the exoteric, and the generally accepted, and the other the Secret Path—the nature of which is explained at initiation.

81. Men ignorant of the esoteric truths and wisdom are called "the living dead."

82. See note 117, verse 306.

83. *Pratyeka Buddhas* are those Bodhisattvas who strive after and often reach the Dharmakaya robe after a series of lives. Caring nothing for the woes of mankind or to help it, but only for their own bliss, they enter Nirvana and disappear from the sight and the hearts of men. In Northern Buddhism, a "Pratyeka Buddha" is a synonym of spiritual selfishness.

84. *Upadhyaya* is a spiritual preceptor, a guru. The Northern Buddhists choose these generally among the *Naljor,* saintly men, learned in *gotrabhujnana* and *jnana-darshana-shuddhi,* teachers of the Secret Wisdom.

85. Yana—vehicle: thus *Mahayana* is the "Great Vehicle," and *Hinayana,* the "Lesser Vehicle," the names for the two schools of religious and philosophical learning in Northern Buddhism.

86. *Shravaka*—a listener, or student who attends to the religious instructions. From the root *shru.* When from theory they go into practice or performance of asceticism, they become *Shramanas,* "exercisers," from *shrama,* action. As Hardy shows, the two appellations answer to the words ἀκουστικοὶ and ἀσκηταὶ of the Greeks.

87. *Samtan* (Tibetan), the same as the Sanskrit *Dhyana*, or the state of meditation, of which there are four degrees.

88. *Paramitas*, the six transcendental virtues; for the priests there are ten.

89. *Srotapatti*—(lit.) "he who has entered the stream" that leads to the Nirvanic ocean. This name indicates the first Path. The name of the second is the Path of *Sakridagamin*, "he who will receive birth (only) once more." The third is called *Anagamin*, "he who will be reincarnated no more," unless he so desires in order to help mankind. The fourth Path is known as that of *Rahat* or *Arhat*. This is the highest. An Arhat sees Nirvana during his life. For him it is no postmortem state, but Samadhi, during which he experiences all Nirvanic bliss.*

HPB note: *How little one can rely upon the Orientalists for the exact words and meaning, is instanced in the case of three "alleged" authorities. Thus the four names just explained are given by R. Spence Hardy as: 1. Sowan; 2. Sakradagami; 3. Anagami, and 4. Arya. By the Rev. J. Edkins they are given as: 1. Srotapanna; 2. Sagardagam; 3. Anagamin, and 4. Arhan. Schlagintweit again spells them differently, each, moreover, giving another and a new variation in the meaning of the terms.

90. "Arrival at the shore" is with the Northern Buddhists synonymous with reaching Nirvana through the exercise of the six and the ten *Paramitas* (virtues).

91. The MASTER-SOUL is *Alaya*, the Universal Soul or Atman, each man having a ray of it in him and being supposed to be able to identify himself with and to merge himself into it.

92. *Antahkarana* is the lower manas, the path of communication or communion between the personality and the higher manas or human Soul. At death it is destroyed as a

path or medium of communication, and its remains survive in a form as the *kamarupa*—the "shell."

93. The Northern Buddhists, and all Chinese, in fact, find in the deep roar of some of the great and sacred rivers the keynote of Nature. Hence the simile. It is a well-known fact in physical science, as well as in occultism, that the aggregate sound of Nature—such as heard in the roar of great rivers, the noise produced by the waving tops of trees in large forests, or that of a city heard at a distance—is a definite single tone of quite an appreciable pitch. This is shown by physicists and musicians. Thus Prof. Rice (*Chinese Music*) shows that the Chinese recognized the fact thousands of years ago by saying that "the waters of the Hoang-ho rushing by, intoned the *kung*" called "the great tone" in Chinese music; and he shows this tone corresponding with the F, "considered by modern physicists to be the actual tonic of Nature." Professor B. Silliman mentions it, too, in his *Principles of Physics*, saying that "this tone is held to be the middle F of the piano; which may, therefore, be considered the keynote of Nature."

94. The *Bons* or *Dugpas*, the sect of the "Red Caps," are regarded as the most versed in sorcery. They inhabit Western and Little Tibet and Bhutan. They are all Tantrikas. It is quite ridiculous to find Orientalists who have visited the borderlands of Tibet, such as Schlagintweit and others, confusing the rites and disgusting practices of these with the religious beliefs of the Eastern Lamas, the "Yellow Caps," and their *Naljors* or holy men. The following is an instance.

95. *Dorje* is the Sanskrit *Vajra*, a weapon or instrument in the hands of some gods (the Tibetan *Dragshed*, the devas who protect men), and is regarded as having the same occult power of repelling evil influences by purifying the air as ozone in chemistry. It is also a *mudra*, a gesture and

posture used in sitting for meditation. It is, in short, a symbol of power over invisible evil influences, whether as a posture or a talisman. The Bons or Dugpas, however, having appropriated the symbol, misuse it for purposes of black magic. With the "Yellow Caps," or *Gelugpas*, it is a symbol of power, as the cross is with the Christians, while it is in no way more superstitious. With the Dugpas, it is like the *double triangle reversed*, the sign of sorcery.

96. *Viraga* is that feeling of absolute indifference to the objective universe, to pleasure and to pain. "Disgust" does not express its meaning, yet it is akin to it.

97. *Ahamkara*—the "I" or feeling of one's personality, the "I-am-ness."

98. "One who walks in the steps of his predecessors" or "those who came before him," is the true meaning of the name *Tathagata*.

99. *Samvriti* is that one of the two truths which demonstrates the illusive character or emptiness of all things. It is relative truth in this case. The Mahayana school teaches the difference between these two truths—*Paramarthasatya* and *Samvritisatya* (*satya* "truth"). This is the bone of contention between the *Madhyamikas* and the *Yogacharas*, the former denying and the latter affirming that every object exists owing to a previous cause or by a concatenation. The *Madhyamikas* are the great nihilists and deniers, for whom everything is *parikalpita*, an illusion and an error in the world of thought and the subjective, as much as in the objective universe. The *Yogacharas* are the great spiritualists. *Samvriti*, therefore, as only relative truth, is the origin of all illusion.

100. Lhamayin are elementals and evil spirits adverse to men and [thus] their enemies.

101. *Jnana Marga* is the "Path of Jnana," literally; or the Path of pure knowledge, of *Paramartha* or (Sanskrit) *Svasamvedana*, "the self-evident or self-analyzing reflection."

102. See note 49, verse 114. "Diamond Soul" or *Vajradhara* presides over the *Dhyani-Buddhas*.

103. This is an allusion to a well-known belief in the East (as in the West, too, for that matter) that every additional Buddha or Saint is a new soldier in the army of those who work for the liberation or salvation of mankind. In Northern Buddhist countries, where the doctrine of *Nirmanakayas*—those Bodhisattvas who renounce well-earned Nirvana or the *Dharmakaya* vesture (both of which shut them out forever from the world of men) in order to invisibly assist mankind and lead it finally to Paranirvana—is taught, every new Bodhisattva or initiated great Adept is called the "liberator of mankind." The statement made by Schlagintweit in his *Buddhism in Tibet* to the effect that *Prulpai Ku* or *Nirmanakaya* is "the *body* in which the Buddhas or Bodhisattvas appear upon earth to teach men"— is absurdly inaccurate and explains nothing.

104. A reference to human passions and sins which are slaughtered during the trials of the novitiate, and serve as well-fertilized soil in which "holy germs" or seeds of transcendental virtues may germinate. Pre-existing or innate virtues, talents, or gifts are regarded as having been acquired in a previous birth. Genius is without exception a talent or aptitude brought from another birth.

105. *Titiksha* is the fifth state of Raja Yoga—one of supreme indifference; submission, if necessary, to what is called "pleasures and pains for all," but deriving neither pleasure nor pain from such submission—in short, the be-

coming physically, mentally, and morally indifferent and insensible to either pleasure or pain.

106. Sowani is one who practices *sowan*, the first path in *Dhyana*, a Srotapatti.

107. "Day" means here a whole *Manvantara*, a period of incalculable duration.

108. Mount Meru, the sacred mountain of the gods.

109. In the Northern Buddhist symbology, *Amitabha* or "Boundless Space" *(Parabrahm)* is said to have in his paradise two Bodhisattvas—Kwan-shi-yin and Tashishi—who ever radiate light over the three worlds where they live, including our own [see note 110 below], in order to help with this light (of knowledge) in the instruction of Yogis, who will, in their turn, save men. Their exalted position in Amitabha's realm is due to deeds of mercy performed by the two, as such Yogis, when on earth, says the allegory.

110. These three worlds are the three planes of being: the terrestrial, the astral, and the spiritual.

111. The "Guardian Wall" or the "Wall of Protection." It is taught that the accumulated efforts of long generations of yogis, saints, and adepts—especially of the Nirmana-kayas—have created, so to say, a wall of protection around mankind, which wall shields mankind invisibly from still worse evils.

112. *Klesha* is the love of pleasure or of worldly enjoyment, evil or good.

113. *Tanha,* the will to live, that which causes rebirth.

114. This "compassion" must not be regarded in the same light as "God, the divine love" of the Theists. Compassion stands here as an abstract, impersonal law whose nature, being absolute harmony, is thrown into confusion by discord, suffering, and sin.

115. In the Northern Buddhist phraseology all the great arhats, adepts, and saints are called Buddhas.

HPB note: *Thegpa Chenpoido,* "Mahayana Sutra," Invocations to the Buddhas of Confessions," Part 1, iv.

116. A Bodhisattva is, in the hierarchy, less than a "perfect Buddha." In the exoteric parlance these two are very much confused. Yet the innate and right popular perception, owing to that self-sacrifice, has placed a Bodhisattva higher in its reverence than a Buddha.

117. This same popular reverence calls "Buddhas of Compassion" those Bodhisattvas who, having reached the rank of an Arhat (i.e., have completed the fourth or seventh Path), refuse to pass into the Nirvanic state or "don the Dharmakaya robe and cross to the other shore," as it would then become beyond their power to assist men even so little as karma permits. They prefer to remain invisibly (in spirit, so to speak) in the world, and contribute toward man's salvation by influencing them to follow the Good Law, i.e., lead them on the Path of Righteousness. It is part of the exoteric Northern Buddhism to honor all such great characters as saints, and to offer even prayers to them, as the Greeks and Catholics do to their saints and patrons; on the other hand, the esoteric teachings countenance no such thing. There is a great difference between the two teachings. The exoteric layman hardly knows the real meaning of the word *Nirmanakaya*—hence the confusion and inadequate explanations of the Orientalists. For example, Schlagintweit believes that *Nirmanakaya* means the physical form assumed by the Buddhas when they incarnate on earth—"the least sublime of their earthly encumbrances" (vide *Buddhism in Tibet*)—and he proceeds to give an entirely false view on the subject. The real teaching is, however, this:

The three Buddhic bodies or forms are styled:

1. *Nirmanakaya*
2. *Sambhogakaya*
3. *Dharmakaya*

The first is that ethereal form which one would assume when, leaving his physical, he would appear in his astral body—having in addition all the knowledge of an Adept. The Bodhisattva develops it in himself as he proceeds on the Path. Having reached the goal and refused its fruition, he remains on earth, as an Adept; and when he dies, instead of going into Nirvana, he remains in that glorious body he has woven for himself, invisible to uninitiated mankind, to watch over and protect it.

Sambhogakaya is the same, but with the additional luster of "three perfections," one of which is entire obliteration of all earthly concerns.

The Dharmakaya body is that of a complete Buddha, i.e., no body at all, but an ideal breath: consciousness merged in the Universal Consciousness, or Soul devoid of every attribute. Once a Dharmakaya, an Adept or Buddha leaves behind every possible relation with, or thought for, this earth. Thus, to be enabled to help humanity, an Adept who has won the right to Nirvana, "renounces the Dharmakaya body" in mystic parlance; keeps, of the Sambhogakaya, only the great and complete knowledge, and remains in his Nirmanakaya body. The esoteric school teaches that Gautama Buddha with several of his Arhats is such a Nirmanakaya, higher than whom, on account of the great renunciation and sacrifice to mankind, there is none known.

118. Myalba is our earth—pertinently called "Hell," and the greatest of all hells, by the esoteric school. The esoteric doctrine knows of no hell or place of punishment

other than on a man-bearing planet or earth. *Avichi* is a state and not a locality.

119. Meaning that a new and additional savior of mankind is born, who will lead men to final Nirvana, i.e., after the end of the life cycle.

120. This is one of the variations of the formula that invariably follows every treatise, invocation, or instruction — "Peace to all beings," "Blessings on all that lives," and so forth.

QUEST BOOKS
are published by
The Theosophical Society in America,
Wheaton, Illinois 60189-0270,
a branch of a world fellowship,
a membership organization
dedicated to the promotion of the unity
of humanity and the encouragement of the study
of religion, philosophy, and science, to the end that
we may better understand ourselves and our place
in the universe. The Society stands for complete
freedom of individual search and belief.
For further information about its activities,
write, call 1-800-669-1571,
e-mail olcott@theosophia.org,
or consult its Web page:
http://www.theosophical.org

*The Theosophical Publishing House
is aided by the generous support of
THE KERN FOUNDATION,
a trust established by Herbert A. Kern
and dedicated to Theosophical education.*